THINKING LIKE A WRITER

A Lawyer's Guide to Effective Writing and Editing

THINKING LIKE A WRITER

A Lawyer's Guide to Effective Writing and Editing

by
Stephen V. Armstrong
and
Timothy P. Terrell

Library of Congress Cataloging-in-Publication Data

Armstrong, Stephen V.
    Thinking like a writer: A lawyer's guide to effective writing and editing/
by Stephen V. Armstrong and Timothy P. Terrell.
        p. cm.
    Includes index.
    ISBN 0-87632-898-2
    1. Legal composition 2. Legal composition—Editing.
I. Terrell, Timothy P., 1949– . II. Title.
KF250.A76 1992
808' .06634—dc20
                                                          92-15739
                                                          CIP

About the Authors

Stephen V. Armstrong is Director of Professional Development and Training at the law firm of Shearman & Sterling. He studied at Yale College and the State University of New York at Buffalo. Before joining Shearman & Sterling, he worked as a reporter and editor for *The Washington Post* and taught literature and writing at the University of Alabama. For the past decade, he has taught many writing programs around the country for lawyers and for federal and state judges. Under a grant from the State Justice Institute, he recently developed materials for writing programs for state appellate judges.

Timothy P. Terrell is a Professor of Law at Emory University School of Law, and also has served as Director of Professional Development at King & Spalding. He has an undergraduate degree from the University of Maryland, a J.D. from Yale University Law School, and a Diploma in Law from Oxford University. He has published books and articles primarily in the areas of constitutional law and jurisprudence. He has conducted numerous programs for law firms and bar organizations on legal writing, professionalism, and law firm training.

Introduction

GOOD WRITING ARISES partly from qualities that cannot be taught: talent, experience, stamina, the spark that sometimes leaps between mind and subject matter. Good professional writing, however, is primarily a craft, not a mystery. It is fashioned from methods that can be learned and practiced separately and, in time, combined to form a skill larger than the sum of its parts.

This book describes the most important of these methods. But its approach is unusual enough to warrant some explanation.

Many books about legal writing claim, at least implicitly, that lawyers as a class write badly. We disagree. Some types of legal writing, it is true, deserve their notoriety. Such things as contracts, statutes, and jury instructions suffer from conventions about their style that often turn them into mazes. And some lawyers can mangle even a simple letter, either because they never learned to write adequately or because they imitate bad models. In general, though, when lawyers write memoranda and letters and briefs, they write no worse and perhaps a little better than most other professional classes. They need help not because they start with a failing grade, but because they face a difficult task: writing clearly and persuasively about complicated matters in situations where a slip can have drastic consequences. For this, the skills developed through the normal course of an education will not be enough. The difference between good school writing and good legal writing is like the difference between a classroom discussion and an oral argument before a judge. The skills that are adequate for the first are only the starting place for the second.

We take our audience, then, to be those who already write decently, perhaps well, but who aspire to something more: a mastery of the craft in which they can take as much pride as they do in their mastery of other, more strictly legal skills. Moreover, we assume that this audience realizes the importance—indeed, the responsibility—of passing on their skill to others.

This is an unusually optimistic approach for a book on legal writing, but we think the optimism is realistic. In fact, lawyers bring a unique asset to the task of learning to write well, an asset most overlook but we shall emphasize. That advantage is their skill in legal reasoning. This claim may be surprising, because some aspects of legal reasoning—fanatical pursuit of precision and thoroughness, reliance on subtle distinctions, tolerance for complication—are often blamed for the worst qualities of legal writing. To say that someone "thinks like a lawyer" is usually a compliment (perhaps grudging) for an intellect that is both finely tuned and very tough, but to say someone "writes like a lawyer" is usually an insult. Lawyers too often accept this insult as inevitable. Their pessimism seems to take this form: Legal writing should be precise, but its medium—language—is slippery and ambiguous. To make language serve their purposes, lawyers must wrestle mightily with it, often twisting it far out of its normal, idiomatic shape. From this it seems to follow that lawyers are caught in a dilemma: If they think like lawyers, they must write prose that is painful to read. If they write clearly, on the other hand, it can only be because they are thinking simplistically.

These assumptions, all the more imbedded because they are seldom articulated, are wrong. It is possible to write precisely about complex matters and to write clearly at the same time. (In fact, if we try to write precisely without writing clearly, we will fail at both: In the long run, we achieve precision by trying to make our meaning clear to someone else.) When lawyers fail the test of clarity, they should not blame their subject matter. The fault lies elsewhere. As we have said, it takes more than ordinary skill to write clearly about complicated analyses. Much of your legal education—and acculturation—does not foster this skill, and many lawyers never take the trouble to develop it. Some positively resist doing so because they take comfort from convoluted writing: An obscure sentence seems to erect bulwarks around the thought it contains, protecting it from attack.

If a lawyer can overcome this psychological obstacle, then his training in legal reasoning gives him a head start in learning how to write clearly about complicated matters.* It does so for two reasons.

---

* Contemporary writers face a new problem: choosing a singular pronoun to refer to a generic human being. Traditionally, of course, writers have assumed that this person is masculine, but a currently popular response to this chauvinism is to assume the opposite. Some writers try for a middle ground, using a variety of techniques: making

First, lawyers develop an unusual degree of analytic sophistication, a combination of conceptual rigor and a logician's equivalent of street smarts. More than most other professionals, they know how hard it is to pin down a concept, how easy it is to miss a crucial distinction, how much work it takes to lay the map of reason over the shifting terrain of human behavior and thought. They know, for example, that the cases in any controversial area of the law are flexible, malleable, and often disconcertingly inconsistent and competitive. Yet despite these difficulties, lawyers are forbidden to relax their standards. They must continue to strive for precision, and to act on the belief that concepts and language, skillfully used, can provide both coherent judgment of past conduct and coherent guidance for future conduct. In this effort to impose a useful structure on complex data, with full awareness of how rigorous the structure should be and how messy the data may be, legal reasoning sets about a task that is more like the act of writing than most other kinds of professional reasoning.

Second, and as a result of their analytic skills, lawyers develop a sophisticated sense of how to undertake an intellectual activity where they must be guided neither by personal taste nor by rigid rules, but by a mix of general principles, precise rules, and all the species of guideline that fall in between. Good lawyers know more than rules and cases. They also understand the basic principles that shape whole areas of the law, principles that push specific cases in predictable directions by organizing and reconciling arguments and information. And, even beyond this understanding, they also grasp the complex relationship among principles themselves, which sometimes conflict and compete. With this perspective, they avoid becoming lost among the dizzying array of narrower rules, precedents, and regulations that issue from the principles.

As writers, lawyers need the same kind of sophisticated understanding about the nature of the guidance they can hope to find. The analogy between writing and lawyering is really quite direct: Both require a grasp of basic principles and of the relationship between principles and their specific applications.

But lawyers seldom see this similarity. Again and again in our conversations with lawyers about their writing, we have been struck by how difficult

---

all references plural ("they"), or genderless ("one"), or neutral ("he or she"), or switching between masculine and feminine at each new example, or using a new coinage ("s/he"). We have reached our own imperfect compromise. We will use the plural whenever we can; when style or grammar require the singular, we will use the masculine in the first half of the book and the feminine in the second.

they find it to describe the methods by which they move from a vague goal—clarity, say—to a specific arrangement of words on the page, and how often, as a result, they seize upon an oversimplified "rule" to guide them. When they describe the advice they have taken from others and tried to follow, what usually emerges is a grab bag of relatively superficial and narrow command-ments such as "write short sentences," "don't use jargon," and "avoid the passive voice"—all jumbled together in no particular order. Compared to lawyers' understanding of the law, their understanding of writing remains primitive. As a result, they find it unnecessarily difficult to improve their writing and, if they supervise other writers, even more difficult to teach them how to improve.

We seek to change this situation by adding to your experience and skill as a writer a deeper understanding of the principles that shape effective written communication. The best professional writing, and certainly the best editing, springs from a thorough understanding of these principles. A few writers, those who have written and read copiously and energetically since childhood, de-velop this understanding without any formal teaching and without being able to articulate the principles they follow. But most of us are not so fortunate. If we are to write as well as we can, we need to think again about the principles that should guide us.

In this book, then, while we will provide specific advice and even something akin to commands, we will ask you first to think about the principles of effective written communication. Among its other advantages, this approach alone helps to develop a writer's most powerful tool: the flexible, perceptive judgment, remarkably similar to legal judgment, that allows him to see and to pick intelligently among the choices of style and organization he faces as he writes. Only from this vantage point can he make the best use of advice about specifics.

Because it emphasizes principles, this book speaks to a wide audience, including both those new to legal writing and those with substantial experi-ence. We realize, however, that not everyone will be in the mood for a survey of principles. There are times in our progress with any craft—or sport, or art—where what we want most is a quick fix or two, to cure a nagging problem or to raise our confidence before we try more arduous improvements. The golfer with a wicked slice wants it cured before he remakes his entire game; the out-of-shape workaholic needs first some simple advice that does not disrupt his life ("Walk half an hour each evening"). Use the book as you need to. The table of contents and index will guide you to solutions to specific problems. At some point, though, we hope you will absorb the principles discussed in the early chapters, because only the principles can finally make you a master of the craft.

Understanding the principles is especially important because lawyers seldom work alone. Most now work in offices where more experienced attorneys supervise newer ones. The novices often complain, however, that, when their supervisors edit their writing, the results are eccentric in method and erratic in quality. Our own observations bear this out. In this context, then, "mastery" of writing means something larger than the ability to write well. It includes the ability to edit the work of others and, equally important, to explain your revisions so that the writer learns from the experience and improves his next product. To do this, you must base your editing on a coherent set of principles and be able to teach them to someone else.

Although the table of contents outlines the book's approach, more information about its organization may be useful. Oddly enough, some readers may want to start by jumping to Appendix A, in which we argue the case for writing instruction even for experienced lawyers. Since you have already read this far, we doubt that you need this advice, but it might be helpful in persuading others who remain skeptical about such programs for the well-educated (or at least much-educated).

The book itself begins with a summary of the principles and techniques it describes. You might find it useful to read the summary first just to get a feel for the book's approach, even though some of the advice will remain cryptic until you read the later chapters.

Chapter 1 is the most fundamental (and therefore the most abstract) portion of the book. It establishes the link between writing and legal reasoning, and discusses the basic tenets of all good legal writing.

Each of the following chapters starts with principles and then goes on to describe the techniques through which these principles work.

Chapter 2 focuses on the context—the audience and purpose—of the project that requires you to write. It is concerned with how thoroughly you understand what you should be trying to accomplish.

Chapter 3 is devoted to large-scale organization: the principles of organizing a document as a whole and its major sections. It begins by describing the process by which readers grasp written information, a process that imposes demands on your organization that go beyond the need for simple logical coherence. The first two sections of this chapter identify two principles on which all forms of organization rely, and the third section develops these principles into seven techniques that implement them.

Chapters 4 through 7 move from "macro" to "micro," from the document as a whole to its parts: paragraphs, sentences, words, and even punctuation. The general principles that guided large-scale organization will also guide us here. The principles of good writing work at all levels.

In Chapter 8, the focus changes from the clarity and persuasiveness of your prose to its character, vitality, and gracefulness—in other words, to its style.

Chapter 9 discusses the process of editing both your own writing and that of others, especially colleagues. Much of the book's advice is intended to be applied when you edit, but this chapter deals with the process itself rather than the specific types of changes you might make as you revise.

Finally, Chapter 10 pulls together, and extends, many of the points made earlier by focusing on the writing and editing of memoranda, briefs, judicial opinions, and letters.

Table of Contents

Summary of
Principles & Techniques of
Effective Writing and Editing

Good legal writing should be:
- – precise,
- – efficient,
- – memorable, and
- – persuasive

❖   ❖   ❖   ❖   ❖

Preparing to write should be like preparing to negotiate.

Determine whether you have more than one audience.

Determine what your audience already knows.

❖   ❖   ❖   ❖   ❖

❖   ❖   ❖   ❖   ❖

❖   ❖   ❖   ❖   ❖

❖   ❖   ❖   ❖   ❖

❖   ❖   ❖   ❖   ❖

❖   ❖   ❖   ❖   ❖

❖   ❖   ❖   ❖   ❖

CHAPTER **1**

Writing and Reasoning: The Basic Connections

WE BEGIN, AS WE PROMISED, with fundamentals: not with advice about writing, but with the nature of that advice. We start here because, as we argued in the Introduction, a writer who wants to improve must understand the principles of the craft, not just random pieces of good advice. An audience with legal training, we said, should be better able than most to benefit from this approach.

If you are in no mood at this point for theory, skip this Chapter and go on to the specifics in later chapters. But come back to this one at some point.

The first section below develops our general proposition: The principles of good writing are best understood as analogous to legal principles—as opposed to legal "rules"—that form the foundation of a lawyer's thought process. Principles, as we will see, can compete with each other, but that contest will be governed by certain fundamental standards. In the second section, we identify two such standards for effective legal writing.

Relying on Principles, Not Rules

One feature of legal reasoning has a pernicious tendency. For practical reasons, the training of lawyers focuses on arguments that will matter to a judge (who has been similarly trained). In this context, something less than all possible arguments will "matter"—for example, some might be dismissed quickly as "moral" or "political" rather than truly "legal." From this lesson, novice lawyers too often draw the strained conclusion that where clearly enforceable rules do not govern, results are simply a function of judicial discretion.

Although most lawyers quickly outgrow this tendency to divide the legal world between "rules" and "discretion," they often retain this naive dichotomy in their attitudes toward writing. They will frequently treat advice about writing as either a rigid rule ("All good writing consists of short sentences!") or a trivial matter of personal taste in which adjudication will not resolve disputes ("Some people like long sentences; I happen to like short ones."). In fact, very little of this guidance rises to the level of a "rule" that would be enforced by a court of language. (The few exceptions include, for example, the rules of grammar and some rules of usage where a clear consensus about "right" and "wrong" has been established.) The vast bulk of advice about writing—particularly about good writing—lacks hard and clear authority.

But that does not mean that we leave reason behind. Lawyers understand this about the law. They realize that what lies beyond the realm of clean, crisp legal rules is not chaos: Even in the gray area of nuance and tendency, rational analysis still applies. If lawyers applied to writing the analytic standards they employ in legal reasoning, they would realize that professional development in both contexts depends upon moving beyond any simplistic dualism between hard rules and unfettered discretion. In both activities, we spend most of our effort in a realm where reasoned judgment is possible even though there are few fixed rules.

One legal theorist has become famous for his attempt to move legal reasoning beyond its traditional "rule-bound" limitations, and we will use his effort as an analogy for our approach to legal writing. Professor Ronald Dworkin has argued that lawyers must distinguish between legal "rules" and legal "principles."* Rules are characteristically narrow, rigid, and obligatory, while principles are broad, flexible, and compelling rather than compulsory. They guide a court generally toward the proper resolution of a dispute rather than dictating a specific answer. Although principles are more abstract and controversial than rules, they are nevertheless, Dworkin argues, part of the system of law relevant to any court.

By the same token, the "law" of good writing does not consist solely of discrete, confining rules, but includes as well background principles that establish the framework within which all rules (and what we will call "tech-

---

* R. Dworkin, *Taking Rights Seriously* (1976). This is, of course, a very quick summary of Professor Dworkin's complex and ambitious legal theory.

niques") apply. Because these principles speak to fundamental purposes, they are the glue that holds together the entire endeavor. They give us the means to assess the relative importance of specific rules (and techniques), to choose among them when they conflict, and to draw them together toward the single end of clear, persuasive prose. Unless we understand these organizing principles, we cannot apply any advice intelligently.

Principles, however, do not work as simply as rules. Because rules are narrow, they provide relatively clear and uncontroversial guidance. In contrast, a legal principle, such as "a person should not profit from his own wrong," is abstract enough that reasonable people can disagree about the conclusions it yields in particular circumstances. The same is true of writing principles. Their application calls for judgment, and judgments may differ.

Take, for instance, a relatively simple principle such as "The structure of a sentence should emphasize what needs to be emphasized and de-emphasize what does not." When two editors apply this principle to a sentence, they may disagree not only about what needs to be emphasized, but also—once they settle that argument—about which methods of emphasis work best. (We discuss these methods in Chapter 5.) This disagreement does not mean, however, that the principle has failed. Out of the many ways in which the sentence could be written, the editors have been able to discard most, settle on a couple, and conduct a reasoned argument about which is best. In writing, as in most professional tasks, it is by this process that we prove our skill, not by the ability to reach a mathematically determinate solution to every problem.

To further complicate matters, principles can conflict and compete. While the principle of "no profit from one's wrong" suggests that a murderer should not inherit the estate of his victim, a prior case in some jurisdiction might have held otherwise. When a judge in that state confronts a new case raising this issue, he would then be forced to choose between the "no profit" principle and another basic principle: "treat like cases alike," or *stare decisis*. Similarly, in writing, a principle such as "Take account of your audience's expectations" may conflict with another principle, such as "Give your readers the gist of your analysis before you embark on the details." On occasion, your analysis may lead to a conclusion so far removed from the one your audience expects that you will be more persuasive if you reveal the analysis only piece by piece—even though that detective-story approach is harder for a reader to follow.

Choosing Among Competing Principles: Two Fundamental Standards

When principles conflict, we need a standard by which to judge their relative importance. In both law and writing there may be no single standard that governs the whole enterprise. Within a part of it, however, at least if it is a simpler part, we can generally find one or two standards to guide us. This book is concerned with one kind of writing: expository prose that explains a legal analysis.* For this genre, we propose two complementary standards by which principles can be assigned their proper weight.

The first is *effective transfer of information*. To convey information effectively, expository writing must be:

❖ *Precise.* It must impart the right information, not just an approximation.

❖ *Efficient.* It must present information so that the reader understands it as quickly as its complexity permits.

❖ *Memorable.* It must express information so that the reader will remember it.

For lawyers, precision is the most important of these qualities, and the one their education emphasizes. This book emphasizes the other two, in which lawyers seldom receive adequate training.

The second standard is *persuasiveness*. As it is usually defined, persuasiveness matters only for writing that advocates a position. But this definition is too narrow. Even in noncontentious situations, most expository writing should be persuasive because lawyers usually want to do more than just communicate information. They want their writing to have an effect in the real world—to help a client make an informed choice, for example, or to guide him

---

* The genre includes letters, memoranda, briefs, and judicial opinions, each of which we discuss in Chapter 10. For our purposes, it does not include documents such as contracts and statutes. In most cases, of course, these documents also have an expository intent: Consumer contracts in particular must explain a situation, not just record an agreement. As a result, some of this book's advice applies to drafting. But drafting is also guided by other principles that we do not discuss. The principle of consistent reference, for example, often requires that exactly the same word or phrase be used to refer to a concept throughout a document. A standard text on drafting is F.R. Dickerson, *Fundamentals of Legal Drafting* (2d ed. 1986).

through a complicated legal procedure—and they also want to establish their credibility. Whether they achieve these ends depends partly on how they write, not just on the raw content of their documents.

Thus, a research memo can "persuade," in this broader sense of the word, if its introduction addresses the reader's real-world concerns and if the lucidity of its organization inspires confidence in its analysis. Even a run-of-the-mill letter to a client about a real estate closing can be persuasive if its organization and choice of words show that the lawyer is looking at this cumbersome ritual through the client's eyes and translating it into his language. If the letter persuades in this sense, it improves the chances that the client will do his part without mistakes, and that he will return to the same lawyer for the next transaction.

So persuasiveness, broadly defined, is a standard all legal writers must face. No matter how sound their reasoning and elegant their prose, they cannot succeed unless, like negotiators, they can shape their work so that it has the practical result they intend—despite an audience that may be hasty, bad-tempered, and quick to judge.

Both of these standards, persuasiveness and the effective transfer of information, imply something important about the nature of expository writing. This kind of writing is communication. Its main purpose is not to leave a record on paper, but to transfer information into a reader's mind. Consequently, to write effectively, a legal writer has to have a working grasp—which means a relatively informal, nontechnical understanding—of how readers process and remember written information. It is not enough to be a grammarian and logician; you must be something of a cognitive psychologist as well.

On the basis of these two fundamental standards, we can list the principles of effective writing in a loose hierarchy that is reflected in our book's organization. It begins with the principles that are most important because they govern the whole of a document or because they apply both to the document's macrostructure (its overall organization) and to its microstructure (the organization of paragraphs and sentences).

As we discuss each principle, we will also discuss the techniques for applying it. In the context of the analogy between writing and legal reasoning, these techniques are the equivalent of more specific legal rules. And, as in the law, each principle will give rise to a variety of techniques, the choice among them depending upon the situation. The techniques are a professional writer's tools, but—to underline again our basic theme—they cannot be used well unless you understand the principles that guide them.

This theme is important enough to be worth emphasizing with two examples before this Chapter ends.

A common piece of advice is to write short sentences. This is not a bad suggestion, since much legal writing suffers from mile-long sentences. But it will not take you very far unless you understand the principle from which it emerges and the other principles with which it sometimes conflicts. In its most general form, the principle is this: "Readers absorb information best when it is broken into discrete, relatively short segments." One way to obey this principle is to write short sentences, but another is to write longer sentences that are crafted into shorter, carefully connected phrases and clauses. If you think only short sentences can be clear, you will have difficulty reconciling this conclusion with some potentially competing principles. To write clearly, for example, you need not only to phrase each piece of information clearly, but also to be clear about the relationships among the pieces, relationships both of logic and of emphasis. Sometimes, it takes a longer sentence to do justice to these relationships. In addition, good writing will vary its rhythms, not as a literary flourish but to keep the reader alert and focused on the content. This variety requires some alternation between short and longer sentences. Unless you grasp these principles, the advice to write short sentences is a clumsy guide to follow—better than nothing, but certainly not advice that will significantly increase your sophistication as a writer.

Here is a second example. Most of us have been taught to avoid the passive voice and use the active, lest we construct sentences such as this: "Undoubtedly jurisdiction of the trial court obtained when the extension of time was granted." Yet avoiding the passive voice is a technique, not a principle, and we cannot apply the technique effectively unless we understand why we should avoid the passive and why, sometimes, we should not.

The passive is dangerous because its use often violates a basic principle for writing sentences: The core of a sentence's content should be stated in its grammatical core. In other words, form and content should match. In a sentence about an action, the core of the content is, in effect, who did what to whom (or to what). To match that content to its form, the "who" should usually go into the sentence's grammatical subject, the "did what" into the verb, and the "to whom or what" into the object. (For example: "The union filed a complaint.") The passive voice often creates a mismatch between form and content: the subject becomes the "to what," the verb carries less meaning or impact, and the object, if there is one, is left to name the "who." ("The complaint was filed [by the union].")

If we use the passive, then, we run the risk of offending against the three fundamental criteria of effective writing: (1) *Precision:* We may leave out a crucial piece of information: whodunit? (2) *Efficiency:* By and large, the active voice produces shorter, simpler sentences. (3) *Memorability:* Readers remember most easily information that has the form of an action ("X did Y"). A writer can help the process of storing actions in memory by using language that makes them explicit.

Avoiding the passive is a means to these ends, however, not an end in itself. At times, other goals may permit—even require—the passive. For example, you may want to construct a smoother transition between sentences, a goal that justifies moving the recipient of an action to the front of a sentence. Or you may want to focus on the victim of an action, or its effect, rather than on the agent: "My client, Mr. Sad Sack, was deeply humiliated by the experience." Or your role as an advocate may lead you to deemphasize who-did-what. In the next example, note that the writer describes his mistake in the passive voice—but the cure in the active voice: "The documents were not included in the initial production through an oversight that we rectified as soon as we became aware of it."

No professional writer will consciously and meticulously go through so complex an analysis each time he decides whether to use or avoid the passive voice. A good writer will have assimilated the principles we have just described to the point that he seldom has to articulate them. But he will base his choices on them nevertheless. This ability to judge the value of a technique on the basis of principle—in other words, to think like a writer—is an ability that all lawyers should develop, and toward which this book leads you.

CHAPTER 2

Understanding the Task:
Audience and Purpose

ALTHOUGH WE ALL KNOW that we must understand our audience and purpose before we begin to write, this point is so obvious it is often taken lightly. Consequently, its usual formulation—something like "Write for your audience"—often does more harm than good because writers think they have understood and obeyed it long before they have. We prefer a different formulation, one that does justice to the complexity of audiences and purposes in legal contexts:

> ❖ **AUDIENCE PRINCIPLE** ❖
>
> *Preparing to write should be like preparing to negotiate.*

No good negotiator starts a negotiation knowing only the identity of his opponent and what he, the negotiator, wants. He also knows as much as possible about his opponent's business environment and background and, most importantly, about his opponent's real needs, as distinct from his explicit demands. For a writer, too, it is seldom enough to know, for example, that your audience is an appellate court and your purpose is to persuade it that a trial court misconstrued a statute, or that your audience is a client and your purpose is to propose a way of reaping greater tax benefits from a business transaction. To understand your task fully, you should look at it from several perspectives, and from each with a sophistication that goes beyond the basic facts.

We list these perspectives below:

❖ **Audience Technique A** ❖

Determine whether you have more than one audience.

For example, are there hidden audiences behind the one to whom your memo (or letter) will be addressed? If you are writing for a more senior colleague, will he send the memo to a client or to another colleague who knows less about the topic? If you are writing for in-house counsel at a client, does he intend to give the memo to his "clients," the business people? If you have more than one audience, which one should determine the memo's content and form? That is, which is your principal target? And how can you address yourself primarily to it and still satisfy the others?

❖ **Audience Technique B** ❖

Determine what your audience already knows.

Both the substance and tone of your document should be dictated by the background your readers bring to it. For example, if your audience is a colleague or in-house counsel, you should consider how familiar he is with the relevant legal and factual background. If he knows a lot, then it is a mistake to write a primer about the basics—as you may be tempted to do if you had to bone up on the basics yourself. If the audience is a foreign client, you should think about how much he knows about U.S. law (and how good his English is). If it is a judge, how much experience does he have with the issues in your case? The goal is to find an approach that is informative without being condescending or wasting time.

❖   **Audience Technique C**   ❖

*Consider which conventions of style and organization will
seem natural to your audience, and which will seem alien.*

Thinking about your audience also means thinking about the appropriateness of your style and organization. Some conventions will seem less familiar and comfortable to your reader than others, particularly if he is not a lawyer.

In terms of style, most lawyers recognize the dangers of unnecessary Latinisms and other forms of legal jargon. But many still use language that is peculiar to the law, and that strikes laypeople as either a little odd or downright silly. Oddities include, for example, most lawyers' insistence on writing "prior to" instead of "before" and, because they dislike apostrophes, writing "the daughter of Smith" instead of "Smith's daughter." In the silly category, the most common offender is the habit of following the first appearance of every named entity with a parenthetical announcement of the short form of its name: "Our client wrote to Ebenezer Trucking and Storage Company ('Ebenezer'). . . ." or worse, " . . . (hereinafter referred to as 'Ebenezer'). . . ." The reasons for this convention are obvious, and in formal drafting it is almost always justified. Like any unthinking habit, however, this one makes strangers laugh when it appears in a place where it has no function. Does the letter refer to more than one "Ebenezer" entity? If not, there is no chance of confusion about what you mean by "Ebenezer." Will your nonlegal audience understand and accept the convention anyway when it pops up at the start of a letter or memo, where you should be establishing the tone of your dialogue with your readers? We would not bet on it—although they will probably chuckle behind your back rather than to your face.

In terms of organization, few lawyers think twice about starting an analysis with an authority (a description of a new case, a quotation from a statute, or the like). Even if, on reflection, they could have imagined a better start, this technique is so conventional that it is taken for granted. Nonlawyers, however, may not know the convention, or be willing to accept it even if they do recognize it. Business executives like to see a memorandum start by stating its point and why it matters. If you start by discussing an authority, even if it is the latest Supreme Court case, your client may feel you are backing towards your point pedantically and tediously.

Style and organization combine to raise another important point about addressing your audience. Thinking about your reader means thinking about the point of view of your analysis—that is, whose "story" you are telling. Note the difference between the following examples. The first takes a legal perspective, telling the "law's story"; the second takes the client's perspective. The first may be appropriate for a judge, an administrative agency, or, on occasion, another lawyer. The second is usually best for the client itself.

> Both the Unruh Act and the Health & Safety Code contain antideficiency provisions. If either of these statutes applies, it will bar the Bank from obtaining a deficiency judgment, regardless of who purchases at the repossession sale. The Unruh Act applies . . . .

* * * * * * * * * * * *

> The Bank will be able to obtain a deficiency judgment against the obligor on the contract if the Bank has made a direct loan to the purchaser of the boat or mobile home. However, the Bank will be barred from obtaining a deficiency judgment, regardless of who purchases at the repossession sale, if the Bank has purchased a retail installment contract from a dealer. The antideficiency provisions are contained in the Unruh Act and . . . .

❖ **Audience Technique D** ❖

Analyze the audience's objectives: What does it want?

On one level, of course, what the audience always wants—or needs, at least—is a thorough, reliable legal analysis. But only law students can (sometimes) safely stop here. Outside academia, the analysis must serve practical ends. If you are writing for a client, the client usually wants advice that will help him achieve a specific end: to make money, solve a problem, get out of trouble, or win a fight. If you are writing for a more senior lawyer, he wants to give the client helpful advice, but also wants to be sure that the advice is sound enough so that it won't come back to haunt him. The first goal will make him impatient with a leisurely, academic analysis that leads to no practical end. The second will make him unhappy with a memo that does not provide all the evidence for (and against) its conclusions, leaving him either to trust your judgment or to do the research himself. If you are writing for a judge, he will want to reach a decision that satisfies his respect for both precedent and justice, but he will probably also want to dispose of the case quickly. (Sometimes, though, he may want help in writing a scholarly, ground-breaking opinion on a novel issue.)

To complicate matters, deciding what the audience wants may often require you to have a sophisticated grasp of its environment and experience, not just its immediate objectives. Is the client's problem a major or a minor one for him? Is his pride involved? If he is in a dispute, does he want to return to good terms with his adversary or to destroy him? Does the law firm partner want a quick, cheap memo to resolve a small issue, or a thorough memo that he can put in the files as backup in case his advice is questioned later?

Once you have defined your audience's needs, make sure the memo's introduction shows that you will fill those needs. Readers will greet everything you write with the same question: "How will this help me?" The answer, in your first pages, should not be "Trust me. Read the next 20 pages and you'll find out." Demonstrate from the start that you are setting out to serve your reader's purpose, not just to write an abstract analysis.

Consider, for example, how a client is likely to respond to the following versions of a letter's introduction:

Version 1

Dear Mr. X:

You have asked us whether, under West Dakota law, ABC's proposed mortgage on XYZ will take priority over a mechanic's lien for certain engineering services performed before the recording of the mortgage.

Under West Dakota law, mechanic's liens are preferred to all other titles, liens or encumbrances which may attach to or upon construction, excavation, machinery or improvements, or to or upon the land upon which they are situated, which shall either be given or recorded subsequent to the commencement of the construction, excavation or improvement. West Dakota . . . .

The statute has been interpreted to mean that any mechanic's lien, whether filed before or after a mortgage is recorded, has priority over that mortgage if construction began before the mortgage was recorded. There is no . . . .

THE CLIENT THINKS: "This guy writes like a lawyer. . . ."

Version 2

Dear Mr. X:

You have asked us whether, under West Dakota law, ABC's proposed mortgage on XYZ would take priority over a mechanic's lien for certain engineering services performed before the recording of the mortgage.

The mortgage would lose its priority only if the engineering services were held to be the start of construction. They probably would not be.

Under West Dakota law, mechanic's liens are preferred to all other titles, liens . . . .

THE CLIENT THINKS: "Probably? I'm supposed to bet our money on 'probably'?"

Version 3

Dear Mr. X:

You have asked us whether, under West Dakota law, ABC's proposed mortgage on XYZ would take priority over a mechanic's lien for certain engineering services performed before the recording of the mortgage.

The mortgage would lose its priority only if the engineering services were held to be the start of construction. They probably would not be, because West Dakota courts have held that a start must involve visible construction work on the site. No West Dakota case has directly addressed this issue for 10 years, however, and more recent cases in other jurisdictions have employed broader definitions of the start of construction. For ABC to avoid risk in this situation, it should revise its proposed mortgage so that it becomes a construction mortgage, the criteria of which will be described in section III of this letter.

THE CLIENT THINKS: "Ahhh, yes."

Of course, few problems lend themselves to so neat a solution. Even when the situation is messy, however, and even when you are writing to a colleague rather than a client, you must show from the start that you are responding to the reader's needs. Here, for example, are two versions of the introduction to an internal memorandum. The writer has been asked whether the opposing party in a litigation can sustain a demand for a jury trial:

Version 1

JONES V. SMITH

FACTS

....

ISSUE

Is an action for unjust enrichment a legal claim, which is tried by a jury, or an equitable claim, which is tried by the court?

CONCLUSION

Both. In many cases, an action for restitution based on unjust enrichment may be brought in either law or equity. Jones' cause of action, however, would probably be considered to be brought in law, and therefore would be tried by a jury.

Theoretically, this may be an adequate answer. Practically, it is not, because it fails to address the real question: On what grounds could we oppose the request for a jury trial, and what are the chances of success? Here is a more satisfying version:

Version 2

FACTS

....

ISSUE

Is an action for unjust enrichment a legal claim, which is tried by a jury, or an equitable claim, which is tried by the court?

CONCLUSION

In many cases, an action for restitution based on unjust enrichment may be brought in either law or equity. Jones' cause of action, however, would probably be considered to be brought in law because his complaint requests only money damages—a remedy at law—and because that remedy would be adequate restitution for his alleged loss.

To persuade a court otherwise, we would have to argue (1) that the case is too complex for a jury's understanding; or (2) that the underlying issue is a breach of fiduciary duty of a kind (such as breach of constructive trust) that is a matter of equity rather than law; or (3) that the court should follow a minority line of cases which hold any action for "disgorgement" of excess profits to be a matter of equity rather than law. None of these arguments is likely to succeed.

In the first version, the writer simply answered the question posed. In the second, the introduction performs another function: It shows the reader how to think about the problem. That is, if we try for a bench trial, as our client wants us to, how would we argue our case? Without this information, the simple answer to the question is incomplete—in fact, frustrating.

More generally, when you cannot offer a clean solution to a problem, you can usually offer a conceptual framework for addressing it. What are the alternatives? What factors should be weighed? Where are the risks and uncertainties? What are the consequences of the possible outcomes? The details belong in the analysis, but the conceptual map should be drawn at the start.

❖ **Audience Technique E** ❖

Analyze your objectives: What do you want?

At one level, of course, you want to provide a thorough, intelligent analysis—in fact, a brilliant analysis—that solves your reader's problem or persuades him to adopt your position. But you usually have a second agenda as well. If your audience is a court or someone with whom you are negotiating, you want to demonstrate your credibility. If it is a client, you may want to show that you can think like a businessperson as well as a lawyer. You may also want to protect yourself, in case the transaction goes bad later, by showing that you exercised all possible care in arriving at a conclusion and in pointing out risks and uncertainties. If the audience is a senior colleague, you want to show that you left no stone unturned.

Often, however, these secondary aims remain half-conscious. As a result, the writer never thinks clearly about how to pursue them—he simply feels an itch that he scratches absent-mindedly. Here are four common rashes:

❖ *Egotism:* We want to impress our readers. There are good ways of doing this and there are bad ways. One bad way is to throw legal jargon at a client. Another is to write forty pages when twenty would do. When these problems occur, it is often because the writer has never said clearly to himself: "I need to impress this audience"—and therefore has never thought clearly about how to achieve that end.

❖ *Cowardice:* We want to stay out of trouble. As a result, we may be tempted to avoid reaching any conclusion for which we could be held responsible. Or, if we have to reach a conclusion, we may bury it in the depths of a memo or letter so that we cannot fairly be blamed if the reader relies on it. Another temptation is to pepper our conclusions with "perhaps," "seems," and the like, using these words not to describe specific qualifications but in the false hope that they lessen our responsibility for the conclusions. If you need to qualify your statements, do so carefully, explaining the reason for the qualification and its consequences for deciding on a course of action. Do not do it by scattering winks and shrugs.

❖ *Greed:* We are reluctant to waste work—or, more bluntly, we want all due credit and more for our hard labor. If this desire is not faced head-on and kept in check, it can lead us to pour all our research and thinking into the final piece of writing, rather than including only what is truly useful.

❖ *Professional arrogance:* We want to sound like lawyers. The wrong way is to load our writing with sentences that look as if they were lifted from a contract or a statute. The right way is to think superbly.

❖   **Audience Technique F**   ❖

Analyze the situation you are writing about:
How reliable are the facts? Could they change?

Make sure you understand which facts you do not know and which ones are likely to change. In law school, the facts on which you base an analysis are usually both adequate and unchanging. At the least, the professor will not change the facts of a hypothetical while you are writing the essay, and without telling you. In the practice of law, however, the facts you are given may be inadequate. Even if you have all you need, they may change as the structure of a deal changes or as discovery proceeds in litigation. Novices often make the mistake of relying too much on unstable or incomplete facts, and trusting that someone will tell them if the facts change.

❖ **Audience Technique G** ❖

Analyze the practical constraints: How much time do you have, and how much effort is the project worth?

Pay attention to deadlines, to the relative importance of the issues at stake, and, of course, to the client's budget. Corporate clients and in-house counsel are increasingly critical of costly over-researching. Your colleagues will also be unhappy if you slow down a transaction or case by making them wait for a long memorandum, especially if you put aside other work in the process.

* * * * * * * * * * *

This list of perspectives, and the questions they provoke, is not meant to be exhaustive. Thinking about your audience and purpose cannot be reduced to running through a formulaic checklist. A list can be useful, though, because it prods you to think more carefully about your approach to a writing task.

This is especially true if you are writing for the first time outside the familiar context of academic audiences and purposes. Yet it is also true for all of us, no matter how experienced, because it is so easy to lose sight of our audience in the act of writing. When we speak, the audience is (usually) directly before us. If what sounds good to us does not sound good to them, we will notice it soon enough. When we write, however, all we see are words. It requires an act of imagination, based on judgment and experience, to understand the effect the words will have on their readers. In this situation, it is easy to think about the audience only cursorily, and to let our own habits and desires take over. It is this danger that leads us to write a table-thumping brief that heaps scorn on our opponent, or a 30-page memo that offers no practical guidance about a client's problem until page 29. If we succumb to this danger, we end up convincing ourselves that our audience really likes what we are forcing down its throat: The client wants the legal jargon because it proves the lawyer is a lawyer; the judge's audience wants his conclusion hidden until the opinion's end because it likes the suspense; the partner wants only an abstract legal analysis because it is not the associate's job to advise the client. As teachers of legal writing, we have heard all these arguments. They are usually signs that the writer has become a solipsist, creating an audience to suit his needs rather than adapting himself to his audience.

None of what we have been saying, incidentally, is intended to imply that you should ever distort an analysis in order to give your audience the answers it thinks it wants. There are times when a client must be told that he cannot do what he wants, or when a court must be asked to rethink its previous conclusion, or when a partner must be told that what he thought was a simple issue has turned out to be a complex one. To serve an audience's true needs is not the same as to cater to its preferences, and it is the mark of a profession that its members refuse to sacrifice the first goal to the second.

CHAPTER 3

Organizing Documents: Why Logic Is Not Enough

WHEN WRITERS THINK about organization, they should be thinking about two distinct kinds: on one hand, the logical structure of an analysis, and on the other, the organization of the writing that presents the analysis. By training and inclination, most lawyers are good at logical organization, for it usually follows the patterns of legal reasoning with which they are familiar. But they are not nearly as good at the other kind of organization. Many never even realize that the two are different, that an impeccably logical analysis may still leave readers frustrated and exhausted because it has not been presented skillfully. The task of the second kind of organization is to make the logic of the analysis as explicit as possible, so that readers see it clearly on the surface of the prose and can follow it easily from the start. This kind of organization relies on the principles of cognitive psychology, not logic, and it therefore requires a different set of skills.

Because it is less familiar, this "cognitive" form of organization will be the focus of the first section of this Chapter. The second section returns to logical organization, not to repeat what you already know about the forms of legal logic, but to point to a trap into which good writers sometimes fall. The third section describes seven techniques for applying the principles of both cognitive and logical organization.

Cognitive Organization: The Principle of Context

To create a cognitively effective organization, you must understand what you are organizing. Despite appearances, it is not a five- or ten- or fifty-page memorandum or brief or opinion. In one crucial sense, those pages do not exist: Unless they are read by someone with a photographic memory, they will never be held as a whole in a reader's mind. At any point, his memory will contain only a few sentences, if that, in relatively precise form. What has gone before will have been winnowed and compressed to fit into his memory, and what is to come is largely a mystery.

You might think, then, that the best way to be clear is to be brief so that you make fewer demands on a reader's memory. Brevity is a virtue, it is true, but it is usually misunderstood, especially in the context of organization. Brevity is not a function of a document's length—the number of its words—but of the time and effort the reader expends to absorb its content. Do you help by adding words or cutting them? In most instances, you should cut them. But in a few crucial instances, you should add them, because by doing so you can provide more explicit—and earlier—information about the structure of your analysis. To understand when you will need to add, you first have to understand a general point about transferring information effectively.

When you organize a document, you are not composing a static structure, a sequence of paragraphs that exists all at once before the mind's eye, like the facade of a building before the physical eye. You are organizing a process: the flow of information through a reader's mind. Moreover, that mind does not remain passive, as if it were a computer database that uncomplainingly tucks away information until the writer decides to punch the "compute" button. As readers, we lack a computer's patience and memory. We read actively, although much of the activity happens in split seconds and never reaches full consciousness. At each moment, we are trying to absorb what we have just read, to figure out how new information connects with old, and to forecast where the analysis will go next. Inevitably, we select some things to remember and discard the rest.

Cognitive organization is based on the fact that this process is not random. To the contrary, we generally remember best what fits together with other pieces of information to form a coherent pattern. Because our memory works in this way, we approach new information by trying to fit it into a pattern. The harder we have to work to make it fit, the less efficiently we read and the greater the chance we will misinterpret or forget the details. Detective stories make us work hard to understand what is happening: We are not supposed to appreciate the significance of the broken watchstrap on the corpse's wrist until much later, when we realize how smart the detective has been—and how stupid we were. With good legal writing, in contrast, we should never have trouble understanding how things fit together as the information flows past.

Hence, the basic principle of cognitive organization:

❖   **ORGANIZATIONAL PRINCIPLE 1**   ❖

*Readers absorb information best if they under-
stand its significance as soon as they receive it.*

One way to grasp this principle is through an analogy. Imagine that the information in your mind is a liquid held in place by a container you have molded for it. This container represents the "significance" of the information, because it is the context within which the information must be understood. If you now attempt to pour your information into another person's mind, it will slosh around meaninglessly unless you first take the time to construct a container in his mind as well. And this container must be a good one: If you concoct it too hastily, it will be only a sieve. This fundamental principle demands, therefore, that you take a step back from the information you are anxious to transfer to gain perspective on it. You will then realize that your first task involves the container, not the liquid.

Here is an example of how the principle applies at the start of a judicial opinion. As you read these paragraphs, pay attention to how you as a reader feel as you work your way through this information.

Original:

This is an appeal from a dismissal of a suit to enforce a compromise settlement and judgment rendered pursuant to the settlement.

Appellant filed a claim with the Industrial Accident Board (IAB) for a work-related injury which he had sustained on October 10, 1970. Dissatisfied with the outcome of that proceeding, and in a timely manner, he filed suit in the district court of Hightop County, West Carolina, to set aside the award of the IAB. On March 17, 1972, the parties entered into a compromise settlement whereby an agreed judgment was rendered in favor of the appellant, setting aside the IAB award and granting him $6,000. Further, as a part of the agreed judgment, the appellee agreed to provide necessary future medical treatment and other related services for two years from the date of judgment.

During the two-year period, appellant made a request for further medical treatment that was refused by the appellee. Appellant then filed suit in district court on the agreed judgment, alleging that appellee's refusal to provide the requested service was wrongful and in fraud of his rights . . . .

At one level, these paragraphs are decently organized: One fact follows another smoothly because the judge has constructed a coherent chronology. Cognitively, however, the paragraphs are badly organized. He has given us no idea about how, and how much, these details will finally matter. Are they just procedural background, or are they relevant to the issues? If so, how? Because we have no context that shows how or what the details signify, we do not know which ones are important. We are therefore forced to dissipate our attention haphazardly over more facts than we can easily remember. As a result, many of us, frustrated and impatient, will skim these paragraphs, knowing that we will have to read them again later anyway.

Consider how much more efficiently—and intelligently—we could have read this passage if we had first seen this context:

Revision:

Appellant, an injured worker, sued in district court to enforce a settlement of a claim before the Industrial Accident Board (IAB), and a judgment based on that settlement. The court dismissed the case because jurisdiction remained with the IAB. We hold, however, that the court had jurisdiction because the case before it was not an extension of the original claim, but instead arose from the wrongful refusal to fulfill a contract.

Now we can understand the significance of what we read in the second and third paragraphs, because we see how some of the details bear upon the jurisdictional issue. When we reach the details of the appellant's request for further treatment and the appellee's refusal, we read them in light of what we have just been told about the distinction between a wrongful refusal to fulfill a contract and an extension of the original claim. In other words, we have been made "smart." Once we understand how the details matter, we are far more likely to focus on the important ones and remember them. We also realize what we can afford to forget—for example, the procedural history leading up to the settlement.

Two more examples of "containers" appear on pages 3–9 and 3–10 (see the revision in both examples). A caution, however: Containers come in many shapes. Do not take our examples as the only models. In particular, a container need not include a conclusion—although, as we will emphasize later, it often should.

This basic organizational principle applies to every level of a document: to the document as a whole, to sections within it, to paragraphs, and even, as we will demonstrate later, to sentences. It is the true justification, for example, for our eighth-grade English teacher's insistence that we start a paragraph with a topic sentence, a rule that at the time seemed like just another form of the adult penchant for telling us to sit up straight and not chew gum in class.

In practice, Principle 1 takes two forms: one when it is applied to give intellectual shape in advance to a new block of information, another when it is applied to link new information to previous information.

❖   **ORGANIZATIONAL PRINCIPLE 1**   ❖
FORM A

Put context before details.

This was the form applied to revise the judicial opinion. As we will show in more detail later, there are two kinds of context: One about the content of an analysis, the other about its structure. The revised opening of the judicial opinion emphasized content ("We reverse . . . because . . .") and not structure (chronological description of facts followed by application of legal principles) because the latter is so common a pattern that it is already a part of any lawyer-reader's "container" of context.

❖   **ORGANIZATIONAL PRINCIPLE 1**   ❖
FORM B

Before conveying new information, first
show its link to existing information.

For convenience, we illustrate this form at the level of a sentence:

Original:

The Fourth Amendment protects citizens of the United States against unreasonable searches by the government. The Supreme Court applies a test that balances a citizen's privacy against the government's interests to determine whether the citizen's rights have been violated in a search.

Revision:

The Fourth Amendment protects citizens against unreasonable searches by the government. To determine whether a search has violated a citizen's rights, the Supreme Court applies a test that balances the citizen's privacy against the government's interests.

In the original, the link between the two sentences becomes clear only at the end of the second sentence; in the revision, it is clear from the sentence's start. As we said a few pages ago, as soon as readers glimpse a new piece of information, they want to know how it fits into your organization. If they have to hold the information in suspense because it has not yet been connected with anything else, then they read more slowly and less efficiently—though they may not understand what is causing the trouble. In our example, where the sentences are short and the link between them is fairly obvious, the benefits of the revision are small. Over several pages, however, the cumulative benefits will be great, especially when the subject matter is complicated.

In sound professional writing, at the level both of the sentence and of large-scale organization, the pattern you will consistently find is "old information → new information," "old information → new information," and so on. The arrow is meant to indicate that the new information emerges from the old in a way that makes the connection between the two immediately clear—and, therefore, shows how the new information fits into the overall analysis. By "immediately," we do not mean immediately *after* the new information has emerged. We mean as soon as it first steps onto the page. Otherwise, the reader will be in the position of an explorer entering an alien land, always a little bemused, a little slow to catch on to what is happening.[*]

---

[*] The "old information → new information" pattern is just as fundamental to the law as it is to communication. The reasoning characteristic of the common law in particular resolves unfamiliar issues by approaching them through analogies to familiar ones.

To apply this principle, you should recognize that "old" information comes in a variety of forms. Some of it is information you are certain your audience possesses before it begins to read. This can range from the very basic, like the meaning of "case law," to the more particular, like the methods by which courts interpret statutes, to the very specific, like the law of fraudulent conveyance. The rest of it is information you give them as they read, so that they approach each new paragraph (and sentence) with a constantly increasing stock of "old" information.

The distinction between the two forms of Principle 1 is sometimes fuzzy, which is not something that bothers us or should bother you. The important thing is to give the reader enough guidance at the right point—a point that comes earlier than most writers think.

Finally, a caveat: This principle must be applied with tact. Your readers will appreciate being guided through your writing, but they are not stupid. If you take them firmly by the hand to lead them around every gentle curve or down every shallow step on the path, they will resent it. But this is rarely the problem with legal writing. Writers, even good ones, usually offer too little guidance, not too much.

Logical Organization: The Principle of Imposed Order

The principle of cognitive organization requires that you make your logic explicit to your readers. To do this, of course, you must start with a sound logical structure. The basic principle of this second form of organization is:

> ❖ **ORGANIZATIONAL PRINCIPLE 2** ❖
>
> *The organization of your material should*
> *match the logic of your analysis.*

This commandment was presumably driven home in college and law school, and we do not intend to run through all the forms of order that college textbooks describe (definition, cause and effect, etc.) or the ones you learned in law school (issue-rule-analysis-conclusion (IRAC), distinguishing cases, etc.). Instead, we want to explain why good writers sometimes fail to follow this basic principle.

The failure does not usually happen when the raw material is a mess, because then the writer has no choice but to think about its organization. The problems arise when the material already has a plausible organization, one that creates a superficial impression of coherence. In these situations, even good writers may fail to realize that existing organization does not match the logical structure of their analysis. As a result, they fail to break free from that organization in order to impose a new one that better reflects their logic. As the word "impose" suggests, this reordering requires willpower.

When we are writing a legal analysis, for example, our authorities will have fallen into some kind of order by the time we begin to write. We may have organized cases by chronology or jurisdiction, or around a key case that others modify, or around a statute they interpret. These and other familiar forms of order, however, are simply means of organizing our research. Legal *writing*, on the other hand, raises a different issue: Will these forms of order also serve as the best means of organizing our report on the *results* of our research? Often they will, although we will need to write an introduction before we plunge into the maze of authority. At times, however, they will not, and these are the occasions when the organization is most likely to go astray. In these situations, the analysis has a logical structure that is quite different from the pattern of the research. The key legal proposition may not emerge until halfway through the sequence of cases, or the sequence may unexpectedly reveal that it had been creating two distinct propositions all along, or a superficially relevant line of authority may turn out to be useless after all.

If we do our job as writers in these situations, we should break free from any organization that does not arise directly from the actual logic of our analysis, whether it is the organization of our research or, to take another tempting trap, the organization used by a writer to whom we are responding. Too often, though, we are tempted to rest comfortably in the arms of the structure that lies ready to hand. If we succumb, we will be asking our readers to retrace the path of our thinking—or of someone else's thinking—rather than offering them a coherent discussion of our results.

Here are two examples of writing that has fallen into this trap. In the first, involving the common situation of a survey of cases, the writer starts by announcing that he will review "a number of recent decisions," then leaves the reader adrift.

EXAMPLE 1

Original:

Although a number of recent decisions have considered the obligations of so-called "successor employers" under collective bargaining agreements, none has dealt with the question of under what circumstances an employer is bound by his predecessor's agreement to contribute and subscribe to employee trust funds. In the absence of direct authority, we must draw what guidance we can from the decisions arising under collective bargaining agreements.

In the first of these decisions, *John Wiley & Sons, Inc. v. Livingston*, the Supreme Court held that . . . .

In *NLRB v. Burns Security Services*, Burns had succeeded Wackenhut . . . .

Burns was followed by *Golden State Bottling Co. v. NLRB*, holding that the Board . . . .

Finally, in *Howard Johnson Co. v. Hotel Employees*, the Court was once again faced . . . .

In concluding that under the circumstances of the case, the successor employer had no duty to arbitrate, the Court in a footnote made the following illuminating statement: . . . .

Revision:

Although a number of recent decisions have considered the obligations of so-called "successor employers" under collective bargaining agreements, none has dealt with the question of under what circumstances an employer is bound by his predecessor's agreement to contribute and subscribe to employee trust funds. In the absence of direct authority, we must draw what guidance we can from decisions dealing with collective bargaining agreements.

As these cases show, the issue cannot be resolved by deciding whether the new employer satisfies a definition of "successor employer" that always entails the assumption of certain obligations. "There is, and can be, no single definition of 'successor' which is applicable in every legal context." [citation] A decision as to which obligations a new employer has assumed must rest on the facts of each case.

In two of the decisions discussed below, the facts demonstrated a substantial continuity of identity between the business enterprises of the predecessor and successor employers. In the other two decisions, ...

In *John Wiley & Sons*, ...

In *Golden State*, ...

In *NLRB*, ...

In *Howard Johnson*, ...

Note that the revision has two parts: It creates an analytical context for the cases, and then it reorganizes their sequence. The same techniques are applied in the next example, where the writer is responding to his opponent's argument. He begins, as many writers would, by attacking the principal authority on which the other side relies. But this organization is not nearly as coherent—and hence, not as persuasive—as using another structure that puts that authority in perspective.

EXAMPLE 2

Original:

ASSESSMENT OF COSTS

Appellant admits that the assessment of costs is a discretionary matter for the trial judge but asserts that, under the particular facts, the trial court abused its discretion.

Appellant relies upon *J. V. Brown Co. v. Smith, Inc.* [citation]. The court there reversed the trial court and relieved the defendant from paying costs where he was not found negligent and had not prolonged the trial. The court held that: . . . .

Revision:

ASSESSMENT OF COSTS

Appellant admits that the assessment of costs is a discretionary matter for the trial judge but asserts that, under the particular facts, the trial court abused its discretion. As the court's opinion demonstrates, however, the court correctly based its assessment on the principle that costs must be assessed in accord with the results at trial.

This principle arises from C.C.P. Article 2198: . . . .

The principle is stated even more explicitly in Comment (b) to Article 2198: . . . .

While appellant rightly points to *J.V. Brown* as an authoritative application of Article 2198, he ignores crucial differences between the facts of that case and of the present situation . . . .

When responding to someone else's argument, as in a reply brief or judicial opinion, the danger of using a plausible but inefficient organization is especially acute. It seems natural to adopt the other person's organization, responding to his points one by one or following his authorities to see if you reach the same conclusion. This approach works if your main purpose is to comment on his analysis. It does not work if you are also trying to substitute a different analysis, as you usually are in a reply brief and often are in an opinion. In this situation, you need to create an organization based on your own logic, rather than letting your analysis emerge (often awkwardly) on the rebound from an organization forced on you by your opponent.

As our examples have shown, the principle of logical organization works hand in hand with the principle of cognitive organization. When the former requires you to reorganize a discussion, the reorganization should include an introduction that provides a better context for the discussion. Conversely, if you make yourself create an opening context in obedience to the principle of "context before detail," you will sometimes find that you also need to reorganize your material. At other times, the two principles actually merge in practice. In order to impose order on your raw material in these cases, it is enough to create an introduction that maps the order, without having to reshuffle the pieces. Here is an example from a judicial opinion:

Original:

The complaint alleges jurisdiction under 28 U.S.C. § 1333 and 46 U.S.C. § 740, which vest the District Court with admiralty and maritime jurisdiction. Callahan argues that the admiralty and maritime jurisdiction does not extend to accidents, like this one, that involve purely pleasure craft with no connection to commerce or shipping.

Callahan bases his complaint primarily on *Executive Jet Aviation, Inc. v. City of Cleveland* [citation]. In that case, the plaintiff, whose jet aircraft sank in Lake Erie . . . .

Callahan suggests that *Executive Jet* requires a significant relationship to traditional maritime activity in all cases, not just those involving aircraft. Several Courts of Appeal have taken this view . . . .

In *Edynak v. Atlantic Shipping, Inc.*, however, the Third Circuit, assuming that *Executive Jet* could be read . . . .

Callahan argues that this discussion in *Edynak* signals an adoption by the Third Circuit of the "locality plus" test for admiralty jurisdiction . . . .

Revision:

The complaint alleges jurisdiction under 28 U.S.C. § 1333 and 46 U.S.C. § 740, which vest the District Court with admiralty and maritime jurisdiction. Callahan argues that admiralty and maritime jurisdiction does not extend to accidents, like this one, that involve purely pleasure craft with no connection to commerce or shipping.

Callahan bases his argument primarily on *Executive Jet Aviation, Inc. v. City of Cleveland* [citation]. In that case, the Supreme Court held that admiralty jurisdiction does not extend to claims arising from airplane accidents unless they bear "a significant relationship to traditional maritime activity." Callahan argues that this test must be applied to all accidents that would otherwise fall within admiralty jurisdiction, and that accidents involving pleasure craft fail to meet the test. We disagree. *Executive Jet's* "locality-plus" test applies only to aircraft accidents. Even if it were to apply more broadly, an accident involving pleasure craft meets the test.

In *Executive Jet*, the plaintiff, whose jet aircraft sank in Lake Erie . . . .

From this point, the revision follows the original.

One qualification to this principle: We have been assuming that it is to your advantage to make your analytical structure clear as quickly as possible. Although this is usually the case, there are exceptions. At times, your position may rest not on impeccable logic, but on a historical trend, or a tension between competing trends, to which your position is an appealing resolution. At other times, your main strength may be the weakness of your opponent's position. In these situations, your work is to engage in a dialogue, not to erect an analytical structure that stands on its own. As a result, it may well make sense to organize a discussion that looks more like the "before" than the "after" in the examples above. But be sure you are making this choice for good reasons, not just because it is the easier alternative.

Seven Organizational Techniques

We now turn to several techniques for applying these principles to the organization of your writing. As you will see, most of them encourage you to front-load your organization: to put more context up front, at the start of documents and of their parts. As we have argued, it is this attention to setting the right context before plunging into details that makes an organization work cognitively as well as logically.

As a mnemonic device, think about organization in terms of the following diagram:

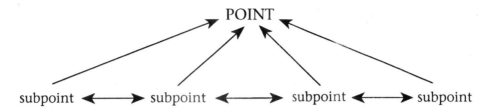

The parts of this diagram suggest seven techniques for organizing your writing effectively.

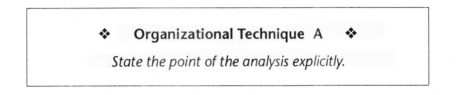

All professional writing attempts to make a point. The point is the basic message, the reason why the reader should read the document. The point therefore includes more than most writers realize. It is not just a "yes" or "no" to a question. It includes, at the least, the reason for the answer. In many cases, it also includes the practical consequences of the answer: How will it affect a business deal or the tactics of a litigation?

Here is an example of the difference between a narrow and a full statement of a point:

> *Question:* Where a bank is agent for a syndicate of banks seeking recovery of defaulted loan payments, may the agent bank sue the defaulting party in its name only as agent without naming the syndicate banks and their subsidiaries as captioned parties to the action?

> *Original Summary Answer:* A strong case can be made for naming only the agent, and not the syndicate for which it acts.

> *Revised Summary Answer [the full point]:* Whether an authorized agent is a "real party in interest" for the purposes of Rule 17(a) remains unanswered by relevant authority. Case law and treatises provide conflicting advice to litigants. A strong case can be made for naming only the agent, and not the syndicate for which it acts. However, because litigation may arise over this issue, it may be more efficient to invest time now in arranging for the syndicate banks to be named as plaintiffs.

For two more examples, look at the last two versions of a letter's introduction on page 2–6 and the two versions of a memorandum's introduction on page 2–7.

The point should be stated explicitly in one place, not scattered in fragments here and there. This advice sounds uncontroversial enough in the abstract, but we find that it meets with a great deal of resistance in practice. The resistance usually takes this form: "If this were a simple issue, I could make the whole point explicit in one sentence (or one paragraph). But it's a very difficult issue, and my analysis is long and complex and full of nuance. I can't sum it up without distorting it."

This resistance almost always rests upon two mistaken assumptions.

One is that you have a choice between making the point explicit or leaving it implicit. In truth, some point will always become explicit; the only choice is whether *you* will make it explicit, or the reader will. At the end of a lengthy analysis, the reader will probably try to sum it up, to make its point explicit as best he can—especially if he has to act on it. If you have not done this for him, you run the risk that he will not see quite the point that you want him to see.

The second mistaken assumption is that, to make the point explicit, you have to make the answer to a question seem more certain than it is. This is not the case. The point includes the degree of probability that attaches to your conclusion, and this needs to be made as explicit as the rest of the point. If the law on the issue is a mess, and the most you can say is that two plausible arguments find limited support in the precedents, then that needs to be—and can be—summed up explicitly. The problem should not be addressed implicitly by sprinkling "perhaps," "possibly," "arguably" and the like through the analysis.

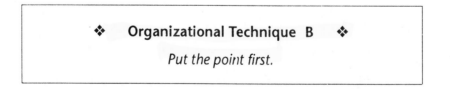

❖ **Organizational Technique B** ❖

Put the point first.

The first technique has a corollary that the examples above imply: Usually make the point explicit before the analysis, not after.

In working through a legal question, a lawyer reaches a conclusion last (in theory, at least). Before reaching it, he will consider the relevant facts and authorities. It is very tempting—in fact, it may feel as if it is the most natural organization possible—to lay out a written discussion in roughly the same order. Start with the question, consider the relevant information and arguments, and finally draw an answer from them. If you do that, though, you confuse two separate acts: reaching a conclusion, and writing about it once it has been reached. The former moves from question to conclusion. The latter should usually move from conclusion to the material that supports it.

Examples of this technique can be found in our earlier discussion on pages 3–9 through 3–10, and they demonstrate that there are at least four reasons for starting with a conclusion. First, as we said in the previous chapter, it gives readers what is most important to them without making them wait. Second, it provides a context that helps them to understand the analysis: If they know where it is heading, they will find it easier to follow its twists and turns. Third, it demonstrates that the writer knows what he is doing, and therefore increases his credibility. Fourth, it encourages better organization in the rest of the document, since it encourages the writer to create a logical defense of the conclusion instead of retracing the path of his research.

Left to follow their instincts, though, most legal writers would split a document's point into its constituent elements, starting with the question and ending with the conclusion. That is easier, certainly, and, to the unskilled or anxious writer, it also feels safer: The conclusion is hidden until a barricade of words has been erected in front of it. To counteract this instinct, some institutions have created official or semiofficial formats that require writers to state all of their point at the start. Many appellate courts require briefs to contain a summary of their argument; most law firms and legal departments require internal memoranda to include a summary conclusion in their introductions. But many writers follow these formats only in letter, not in spirit. As a result, their summary conclusions are too brief. We are encouraging you not only to put conclusions up front, but also to flesh them out so that they summarize your entire point. (Again, look at the example used for Organizational Technique A on page 3–13.)

We also encourage you to lead with a conclusion not just at the beginning of the document, but whenever you start a new line of analysis designed to answer a question. For example:

Original:

Section 16(B) Liability: The ABC Group is also exposed to Section 16(B) liability risk. Since the group will buy 100,000 shares of Megabucks from XYZ, amounting to 15 percent of Megabucks's shares, it may be held liable as persons holding more than 10 percent of the corporation.

The Section 16(B) question revolves around whether there has been a purchase and a matching sale (or vice versa). While it is clear that the ABC Group will purchase Megabucks shares, it is unclear whether there is a matching sale at the time those shares are exchanged for Imperial shares after the merger.

An argument could be made that since Megabucks is the surviving entity with a different name, the stock exchange is merely . . . . Unfortunately, ...

Revision:

ABC Group's Section 16(B) Liability: [first and second paragraphs remain the same]

As the discussion below will explain, the stock exchange will not be a sale if . . . or if . . . . If neither of those conditions is met, however, then the exchange *will* be a sale. Nevertheless, ABC can still avoid 16(B) liability if . . . .

A qualification: Like all techniques, the technique of conclusion-reporting rather than conclusion-finding is subject to exceptions. We suggest not that you always use it, but that—contrary to the habits of most legal writers—you train yourself to assume that you will use it unless there are good reasons otherwise. The most common reason is that the conclusion will be controversial or unpopular or superficially implausible, so that it may be rejected out of hand unless you lead readers to it step-by-step. In this situation, the detective-story organization may work best. But it should be the result of conscious choice in special circumstances, not the normal structure of your work.

To build the habit of starting with a full statement of your point, it helps to imagine a tough and demanding audience—perhaps someone like the journalist for whom one of this book's authors worked as a novice reporter. He was a traditionally abrasive city editor, out of the old cigar-chomping school. When he saw one of his reporters returning from an assignment, he would wave him over for interrogation.

"So wad'ya see?"

"Well, there were maybe a hundred people marching around the building, and . . . "

"No, no! What happened?"

"Well, things were pretty quiet until the police tried to move them back . . . "

"No, no, dummy! What's the big picture, what's it all worth?"

Think of your audience as someone who will blow cigar smoke in your face until you give him the big picture. Then—but not before—he will let you go away and put the details down in peace.

❖   **Organizational Technique C**   ❖

When necessary, link your point to a "road map"
that summarizes the organization of your analysis.

If readers are to grasp the coherence of your analysis as it unfolds, rather than only at its end, then they will have to see not only the point to which it leads, but also the route by which it gets there. And they will have to see this in advance. This summary of your route is often called a "road map."

The more complex, unfamiliar, or controversial your analysis, the more important this technique becomes. But do not be embarrassed to use it even when describing a simple two- or three-part structure. The road map analogy is apt: No matter how clearly the roads are marked at each intersection, a driver will be less anxious if he can look at a map ahead of time. Even a simple map helps:

EXAMPLE 1

This case raises two hearsay issues, one relating to the business records exception and one relating to out-of-court admissions. We will consider each in turn.

EXAMPLE 2

The Division's claim raises three issues. Was an overpayment made? If so, does W.C.S.A 44:10-4(a), and the case law interpreting it, authorize a lien to recover the money? If not, can the Division rely on W.C. Reg. 44.10.(4), which does authorize a lien, despite the lack of statutory authorization?

Road maps demand more care in legal writing than lawyers (characteristically pressed for time) recognize. In complex documents, readers will search for and seize upon any clues the writer tosses out about the unfamiliar terrain ahead. This means that any summary that *looks* like a road map—particularly a list—will be taken as an implicit outline of what lies ahead. If you inadvertently create a misleading map, the results will not be pleasant. While readers may be only subliminally irritated by the absence of a road map, they will be positively annoyed by a false or misleading one.

Here is an example of a misleading map:

> Generally, a court will not second guess a decision made by the directors of a corporation when it can be shown that they acted in an informed manner, in good faith, and in the honest belief that the action taken was in the best interest of the corporation. As will be discussed below, we think that you can show that you have complied with these requirements.
>
> 1. *Good Faith . . .*
>
> 2. *Disinterestedness . . .*
>
> 3. *Due Care . . .*

The author initially suggests a clear three-part analysis: "informed manner," "good faith," and "honest belief . . . best interest." The reader now expects to see these three topics developed, and in that order. Instead, the author divides the document into three sections that correspond neither in order nor apparent substance to the three he announced.

This lesson returns us to familiar fundamentals. If you are going to write for your readers rather than for yourself, you must view your document from their perspective and go out of your way to guide them through it.

❖   **Organizational Technique D**   ❖

In your road map, describe either the
"vertical" coherence of the document or its
"horizontal" coherence, or sometimes both.

As the examples above demonstrated, road maps come in two forms. The first presents subpoints that are each linked to the document's point but not to each other. (See the first example on page 3–17.) We will call this "vertical" coherence, to match the direction of the arrows in the diagram on page 3–13. The second relies on "horizontal" coherence, or the interconnection among the subpoints themselves. This relationship is not simply their sequence. It is the way in which the subpoints—or, on a smaller scale, the lines of analysis within a single subpoint—are bound together logically. (See the second example on page 3–17.) This pattern is often referred to as an "analytical theme," and it constitutes the underlying skeleton of the analysis. A road map ordinarily describes either vertical or horizontal coherence, depending upon the structure of the analysis. But it may cover both if the document is long and complex.

Vertical coherence may seem a remarkably basic topic for this book, but we see it ignored often enough to justify an additional comment. The purpose of being clear about the connection between each subpoint and the main point is to be certain that each of your principal ideas is "to the point," and not in fact one step removed from it. In other words, you might announce in a road map that you will develop your point through three arguments—A, B, and C. This should mean that the analysis could be diagrammed as follows:

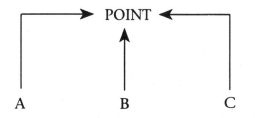

On reflection, though, you may realize that argument B does not speak directly to the point, but instead develops some aspect of argument A:

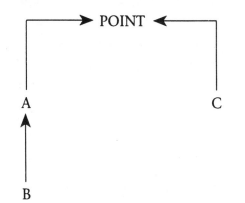

Your road map must therefore be redrawn accordingly.

Attention to vertical coherence will be helpful as you check your reasoning both from the "top down" (that is, does the main point implicate each of the subpoints?) and from the "bottom up" (does each subpoint speak directly to the main point and not to another subpoint?). As you develop each subpoint, you may find it necessary to redraft your road map, and even your point, to ensure that they properly serve their organizing purposes.

Horizontal coherence—the relationship among the subpoints them-selves—may involve countless possibilities, but they fall roughly into two categories. In the first, you establish the logical relationship among the questions, propositions, **or conclusions** that are basic to your analysis. (Again, see the second example **on page 3–17.**) In the second, you establish the analytical procedure by which **you will approach** an issue. This could be, for example, the contrast between **competing bodies** of case law, with each set of cases examined separately—or, **alternatively, with** both sets examined simultaneously in light of each of several **issues. Or** the theme could be the varying results of applying the same law to **different factual assumptions.** At times, the procedure will be so familiar, at least **to a legal reader,** that it does not need to be stated explicitly to be clear, because **the reader already** possesses it as "old" information before he begins to read. **Lawyers need** not be forewarned, for example, about an analysis that moves **from a statute** to the cases interpreting it. The more complex or unpredictable the **analytical** procedure, however, the more important this technique becomes. **And in one** situation the reader is unlikely to forgive you for not using it: when **he has plowed** through three pages of dense case analysis under the impression **that the cases** control, only to discover that you discard this line of cases in **favor of** another or divide it into two distinct lines. The reader will feel misled **and** mistreated, because you have broken one term of your implicit contract **with him:** no surprises.

When you **are faced with** a complex assignment, the analytic procedure or theme may not be **immediately** obvious. In fact, you may have to create it, by the way you cast **the issues.** This work needs special attention, for example, when you write the **summary** of the argument in a brief. In some briefs, the summary consists of **topic sentences** from the brief's sections set down next to each other with **little concern** for whether, once they reside in the same paragraph, they **constitute** a coherent logical pattern. This casualness is always a mistake. The **summary** should not just list the brief's "topics"; it should demonstrate how **they fit together** into a single argument.

The taxonomy **of maps in this section** is meant to help you think about the preliminary work **you should** do before asking your reader to enter the maze of your analysis. It is **not meant to be** exhaustive, and you should not let it limit your ingenuity in **constructing useful** road maps.

❖   **Organizational Technique E**   ❖

Impose clarity on the division and sequence of the subpoints.

In order to **draw a clear** map, of course, you have to start with a diagrammable **system of roads. A** tangled knot is difficult to map. Although legal writers are better trained than most in constructing logical clarity out of chaos, young lawyers in particular are sometimes overwhelmed by the interconnectedness of things. Each issue is pertinent to three others; each point needs to be supported by reference to four others; nothing stands alone. Precisely because a good legal mind is so quick to see connections, it sometimes has trouble imposing a stable, relatively simple order on its writing. In this process, "impose" is the crucial word. While you do not want to oversimplify, you do want to build as simple a structure as possible to support the complexity of the analysis. Each topic and subtopic should be discussed in one place and one place only. There may be cross-references to it elsewhere, but the cross-references should be just that, not further developments. The road system that connects the topics should then be diagrammable: Each topic should emerge clearly from the preceding one, or have a clearly parallel or antithetical relationship to it. If you cannot draw a relatively simple diagram of your topics, you ought to determine why before proceeding. "Relatively simple" means something like the diagrams below.

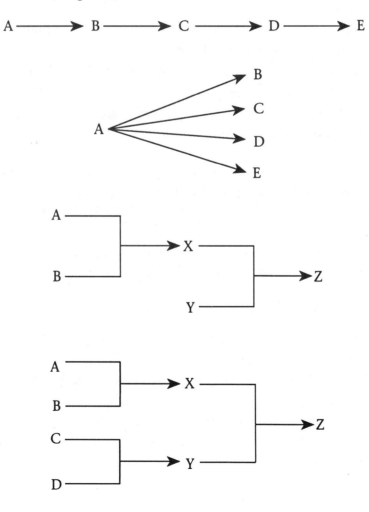

> ❖ **Organizational Technique F** ❖
>
> *When organizing facts, use one organizing*
> *pattern at a time, and make the pattern explicit.*

Early in this chapter, we said that writers are most likely to have trouble organizing a legal analysis not when they start with raw material, but when a deceptively plausible organization is already at hand. In organizing facts, there is a similar danger. Most clumps of facts have a chronological thread running through them, even if they include much more than a simple narrative. Writers are tempted to believe that as long as they return to the chronology occasionally their organization will be clear. If they start in 1970, mention 1973 and 1978 along the way, and end in 1981, they can pack in all kinds of details without losing the reader. They can pause to develop the facts relevant to one issue, then pick up the thread of the narrative, pause again to explain a dispute between two experts, and so forth.

This optimism is misplaced. In organizing facts, a writer must create a clear pattern and follow only one pattern at a time.

There are five basic patterns. You can organize facts according to chronology, actor, issue, witness, or geography. All are self-explanatory except, perhaps, the second, by which we mean a pattern based on the actions of one person or institution. For example:

> Mr. Jespersen opened the business on . . . . He had several discussions with Ms. Tucker about expanding the business, and entered into an agreement with her . . . . He also entered into discussions with . . . .

To organize facts clearly, first make a conscious choice about which pattern to use. Mixing them can be fatal. If you are attempting to establish a chronology and also explain the controversy about two crucial issues, the result is usually—not always, but usually—chaos. There is only one frequent exception to this keep-it-simple principle: The chronological pattern and the one based on an actor often fit together naturally and clearly. If the facts fall into two of the other patterns, most of the time you should use them in sequence, not simultaneously. In practice, this usually means that in complicated situations you should present the chronology first, and then develop specific issues or controversies.

For example:

By chronology:

J. entered first grade . . . .

In 1981, she was placed in . . . .

Two years later, she was moved to . . . .

Then by issue:

Starting in 1980, J. began to exhibit behavior that . . . .

As a result of this behavior, school authorities concluded that . . . .

Then by witness:

On the question of whether her present nonresidential program has resulted in significant educational progress, Dr. Jones stated that . . . .

Ms. Smith, on the other hand, said that . . . .

Even with a relatively brief and simple set of facts, the situation can be made clearer by using one pattern at a time:

Original:

On August 4, 1983, Jessica Hall was involved in a motor vehicle accident at the intersection of routes 6 and 25 and the spur from exit 9 of I-84 in Newtown. Jessica was a passenger in a pickup truck driven by her mother, Wendy Hall. Wendy Hall left exit 9 of I-84 and proceeded eastbound on the exit spur to routes 6 and 25. At this point, routes 6 and 25 overlap into one road. When she approached the intersection of the spur and routes 6 and 25, she attempted to turn left to go north on routes 6 and 25. She testified that because her vision was obstructed by brush, she could not see traffic traveling south on routes 6 and 25 so she inched her way onto the highway to obtain a view. At that point, a tractor trailer driven by John Jones was driving southbound on routes 6 and 25. Wendy Hall did not see the tractor trailer until it was suddenly upon her vehicle. Jones attempted to avoid a collision by braking and swerving to the left but was unable to do so and struck Wendy Hall's truck, severely injuring Jessica Hall.

Revision:

[FIRST, THE CONTEXTUAL FACTS] On August 4, 1983, Jessica Hall was involved in a motor vehicle accident. She was a passenger in a pickup truck driven by her mother, Wendy Hall. The truck collided with a tractor trailer driven by John Jones, and the impact severely injured Jessica Hall.

[NEXT, THE GEOGRAPHY] The accident occurred at the intersection of exit 9 of I-84 with routes 6 and 25. At this point, routes 6 and 25 merge into one road as they are joined by the exit spur. According to Wendy Hall's testimony, the view from the exit spur is obstructed by brush, so that drivers leaving the exit cannot see traffic traveling south on routes 6 and 25.

[FINALLY, THE NARRATIVE] Wendy Hall left I-84 and proceeded east on the exit spur to routes 6 and 25. When she approached the intersection, she attempted to turn left to go north on routes 6 and 25. She testified that because she could not see traffic traveling south, she inched her way onto the highway to obtain a view. She did not see Jones' tractor trailer until it was suddenly upon her vehicle. Jones attempted to avoid a collision by braking and swerving to the left, but was unable to do so and struck Wendy Hall's truck.

After you have chosen a pattern, make it explicit to the reader. The simplest, and usually the best, method is to begin most sentences with words that show how the sentence fits into the pattern. If it is a chronological pattern, in which most sentences will contain a date or time, that information should appear at the start, not somewhere in the middle. If it is a pattern based on one person's actions, that person should usually be the subject of each sentence, and should be referred to near its start. In the following example, the revision combines these patterns:

Original:

In January 1976, Plaintiff went to Defendant for treatment involving the construction and placement of a three-tooth bridge, which Defendant cemented in Plaintiff's mouth on May 12.

Dr. Bright, an associate of Defendant's, also performed root canal work on tooth #1 at the same time. Defendant then referred Plaintiff to Dr. Skillful, who performed an apicoectomy.

Plaintiff returned to Defendant on at least two occasions complaining of discomfort and pain. On these visits Defendant found the bridge to be secure.

In August 1976, Plaintiff also consulted Dr. Drill, who did root canal work on two teeth and placed a five-tooth bridge in Plaintiff's mouth after attempting to re-cement the three-tooth bridge, which he had found to be loose.

Revision:

In January 1976, Plaintiff went to Defendant for treatment involving the construction and placement of a three-tooth bridge, which Defendant cemented in Plaintiff's mouth on May 12.

At the same time as the bridge work, Plaintiff had root canal work on tooth #1 performed by Dr. Bright, an associate of Defendant. In addition, after the placement of the bridge, Plaintiff was referred by Defendant to Dr. Skillful, who performed an apicoectomy.

After these procedures, Plaintiff returned to Defendant on at least two occasions complaining of discomfort and pain. On these visits Defendant found the bridge to be secure.

In August 1976, after the second of these visits, Plaintiff consulted Dr. Drill. He did root canal work on two teeth and placed a five-tooth bridge in Plaintiff's mouth after attempting to re-cement the three-tooth bridge, which he had found to be loose.

❖   **Organizational Technique G**   ❖

Use the first four techniques continually,
not just at the beginning of the document.

We have made this point before, but it is worth repeating. Even writers who are conscientious about "frontloading" their organization at the start of a document often get lazy as the document progresses. They will write a good introduction in the first page or two, and then plunge ahead. But frontloading is important at the start of each new section (whether or not it is formally marked as a section). Think of this as the technique of continual introduction. Take your first introduction to be the map to a country your reader is about to enter, and then remember to provide maps for the cities and towns along the way.

The form of these reintroductions depends upon the situation. At times, you will need to set a new context for the new information—sometimes in a sentence or two, sometimes in a paragraph or two, depending on the size and complexity of the section. At other times, the reader needs only a "road sign" to locate where he is on the map he has already been given: "We now turn to the second of the two hearsay issues." or "Although the statute itself [which has just been discussed] does not authorize a lien, plaintiff claims that the regulation does." Subheadings, of course, can also serve as road signs. Some writers avoid these reminders because they seem simple-minded. The writer, after all, thinks where he is going is obvious. In a long and complex document, however, readers crave these directions because they let them keep a firm grip on the basic structure despite its complexity.

In practice, this continual introductory work is most often slighted not at the formal start of a new section but in its interior. Here are three examples of interior "mini-introductions," each in bold type.

EXAMPLE 1

While these cases present favorable support for our position, the 25th Circuit has declined to follow *Carter*'s holding.

In several decisions, the 25th Circuit has held that a promise of immunity made by a United States Attorney in one district does not necessarily bind a United States Attorney in another district. Instead, these cases have held that an agreement that includes a promise of immunity must be construed in light of its circumstances.

In a 1972 case, *United States v. Smith*, Judge Green listed two factors that limit the enforceability of such an agreement . . . .

In a 1979 case, in contrast, Judge Green upheld an agreement on the grounds that . . . .

EXAMPLE 2

Service of process upon the Secretary of State as the designated agent of a foreign sovereign under state long-arm statutes runs contrary to the congressional intent of the FSIA. If plaintiffs could sue foreign state-owned corporations by service upon the Secretary of State, they could defeat the Act's goal of uniformity and render meaningless the exclusive jurisdictional requirements of Sections 1330 and 1608. And if a foreign sovereign were subject to the varied service provisions of *every* state, there would be confusion over jurisdictional procedures and requirements among foreign sovereigns. This would result in the disparate treatment of foreign entities involved in U.S. lawsuits.

Moreover, details in both the House Report and Section 1608 indicate that Congress did not contemplate service of process on Secretaries of State.

Notably, the House Report on the FSIA expressly states that "[i]f there is no special arrangement [for service of process under Section 1608(b)(l)] and if the agency or instrumentality has no representative in the United States, ..."

Furthermore, within Section 1608, when service of process upon the U.S. Secretary of State is a proper method . . . .

In the next example, in order to provide clearer road signs to guide readers through the passage, the revision takes two steps: It changes the wording of some existing sentences and it adds some new ones.

EXAMPLE 3

Original:

To effect a valid pledge of an intangible chose in action such as a bank deposit, the pledgor must transfer possession of an "indispensable instrument" to the pledgee. *Id.* at 562; *see Peoples Nat'l Bank of Washington v. United States*, 777 F.2d 459, 461 (9th Cir. 1985).

Restatement of the Law, Security § 1 comment (e) defines an indispensable instrument as "formal written evidence of an interest in intangibles, so representing the intangible that the enjoyment, transfer or enforcement of the intangible depends upon possession of the instrument." *See* Annotation, *Pledge by Transfer of Instrument*, 53 A.L.R. 2d § 2 (1957). A passbook that is necessary to the control of the account has been held to be an indispensable instrument. *Peoples Nat'l Bank*, 777 F.2d at 461; *Walton v. Piqua State Bank*, 204 Kan. 741, 466 P.2d 316, 329 (1970). In *Miller v. Wells Fargo*, the corporation did not have a passbook account, but rather gained access to its account by Telex key code. The bank argued that the telex key code was an indispensable instrument because only the bank, and not the corporation, had knowledge of the code . . . .

In *Duncan Box & Lumber Co. v. Applied Energies, Inc.*, 270 S.E.2d 140 (W. Va. 1980), the bank agreed to finance the purchase of land by a subdivider . . . .

Revision:

To effect a valid pledge of an intangible chose in action such as a bank deposit, the pledgor must transfer possession of an "indispensable instrument" to the pledgee. *Id.* at 562; *see Peoples Nat'l Bank of Washington v. United States*, 777 F.2d 459, 461 (9th Cir. 1985).

An indispensable instrument is defined in Restatement of the Law, Security § 1 comment (e) as "formal written evidence of an interest in intangibles, so representing the intangible that the enjoyment, transfer or enforcement of the intangible depends upon possession of the instrument." *See Annot. Pledge by Transfer of Instrument*, 53 A.L.R. 2d § 2 (1957). **Such instruments have been held to include, for example,** a passbook that is necessary to the control of an account. *Peoples Nat'l Bank,* 777 F.2d at 461; *Walton v. Piqua State Bank,* 204 Kan. 741, 466 P.2d 316, 329 (1970). **On the other hand, they have been held not to include a Telex key code.** In *Miller v. Wells Fargo*, the corporation did not have a passbook account, but rather gained access to its account by Telex key code. The bank argued that the telex key code was an indispensable instrument because only the bank, and not the corporation, had knowledge of the code . . . .

The transfer of an indispensable instrument may not be necessary to effect a valid pledge, however, when an account has been set up by agreement between creditor and debtor to secure the debtor's obligations. In *Duncan Box & Lumber Co. v. Applied Energies, Inc.*, 270 S.E.2d 140 (W. Va. 1980), the bank agreed to finance the purchase of land by a subdivider . . . .

Here is a summary of our seven organizational techniques as they relate to cognitive organization: At the start of each argument, each part of an argument, and each chunk of information that goes into an argument, give readers advance information about what they will read. Why is it relevant? What is its structure? Where will it lead? In other words, make your readers smart. This will reduce the time and effort they need to put into reading and increase the chances they will understand, remember, and be persuaded by your arguments. If you refuse them this help, they may move through your prose with no more speed and comprehension than a person walking backwards down a twisting road.

By using these techniques, moreover, you will gain a second advantage. There is no better way of making sure that you yourself understand—*really* understand—your argument. We are all tempted, occasionally, to believe that our logic is so sophisticated, so complexly nuanced, that readers must feel their way through it step by step to appreciate it properly. Resist this temptation. If you are unable to give readers the aids we have described, you need to rethink your argument. If you provide these aids, you will also force yourself to concentrate on the skeletal logic of your writing, the bones that support it, and you will reduce the chances of needless digression.

A final piece of advice: In a first draft, writers rarely do an adequate job with cognitive organization. The struggle with logical organization consumes too much energy to leave much for the niceties of communicating clearly. In addition, because the structure of an analysis usually evolves as it is committed to writing, some of the introductions and transitions in the draft are probably misleading. As a result, you should assume that the organizational techniques described above will need special attention when you revise a draft.

CHAPTER 4

Organizing Paragraphs: Focus, Flow, and Emphasis

WE NOW DESCEND a step in detail to the organization of paragraphs. Our basic premises remain the same, however, because the principles and techniques of good writing are consistent at every level of a document. Consequently, although we will describe some new principles, we will also return to ones from the previous chapter. In turn, the new principles are relevant to large-scale organization, and you should be able to work out their application there without much trouble.

We start with two basic and familiar principles, approached from a new perspective. By themselves, they will get you only to the point of writing adequate paragraphs rather than bad ones. They establish the foundation, however, for moving on to the principles of good paragraphs.

Between a bad paragraph and an adequate one, the difference is usually that the bad paragraph lacks the rudimentary elements of unity and coherence.

> ❖   **PARAGRAPH PRINCIPLE 1**   ❖
>
> *A paragraph should focus on one central topic and organize its supporting points into a logical sequence.*

Rudimentary, but essential: Without unity and coherence, nothing else matters. You have heard this since junior high school, probably, and at this point you are unlikely to let bad paragraphs survive beyond a first draft. If you notice them in the writing of a lawyer you supervise, or if they are pointed out in your own writing, tackle the problem energetically and intensively until it is cured. Readers will interpret it as a weakness in a writer's thinking, not just his writing, and they are likely to pass a quick and harsh judgment on his ability as a lawyer.

In general, though, the problems we see in paragraphs do not arise from fundamental incoherence. They result from the writer's failure to make his logic explicit to his reader. In other words, to use the distinction we created at the start of Chapter 3, the paragraph's organization does not work cognitively, even though it is defensible logically. In paragraphs, this failure can be even more damaging than it is in large-scale organization. Because the scale is smaller, the information comes at a faster pace. As the readers move from sentence to sentence, they have less time to decipher the connections than when they move from section to section or paragraph to paragraph. As a consequence, if you fail to make the paragraph's logic explicit, a reader is more likely to think that the logic itself—not just your presentation of it—is flawed.

To guide readers through a paragraph, Principle 1 above should be applied in two by-now-familiar ways:

❖   **Paragraph Technique 1A**   ❖

At or near the beginning of a paragraph,
provide a context for its information.

Junior high school taught all of us to begin a paragraph with a topic sentence. Because we were new to the game, we wrote some embarrassingly clunky openings. As we became more sophisticated writers, we developed a greater repertoire of ways to provide an opening context. The simple topic sentence is still useful at times:

> In Lower Valdamia, there are no law schools.

At other times, we might turn to a sentence that promises more information, and therefore draws readers into the paragraph:

> In Lower Valdamia, law schools were banned by a 19th-century edict
> against lawyers that is unique in modern history.

Or we may use a sentence that states the paragraph's "point"—the proposition it argues or the conclusion it reaches—as well as its topic. This point may present itself either as a neutral proposition, as in the first example below, or as an argumentative one, as in the second.

> In Lower Valdamia, there are no law schools because the central government fears that they would become hotbeds of agitation.
>
> In Lower Valdamia, the absence of law schools is at the root of the country's political backwardness.

Although the choice among these alternatives depends in part on the paragraph's content, it also depends on the intellectual structure you want to give the paragraph. Should it support a point that is stated completely at the start? Or should it unfold an analysis in a way that leads the reader onto new ground by the paragraph's end? We will discuss this choice in more detail in Paragraph Technique 5A.

As your skill with paragraphs increases, you should develop a sense of a paragraph's normal rhythm: a quick two beats at the start, where you link the paragraph to the preceding one and then establish its new topic; a smooth glide through the middle, interrupted only for the sake of emphasis (see Paragraph Technique 5B); and, often but not always, a concluding beat to extend the point in a convincing or enlightening way. Once you know the basic rhythm, you can improvise the variations.

In practice, lawyers are most likely to omit an adequate topic sentence at a paragraph's start when they discuss cases or other authorities. We flinch when we come upon a paragraph that begins: "In *Smith v. Jones* [citation], the plaintiff broke his leg while attempting to hang-glide from the Verrazano Bridge." Eventually, we will discover what point the writer draws from the case, but it will take a while. Do not fall into this habit. State the point first.

In addition to needing topic or "point" sentences, paragraphs may also require road maps and road signs. In the paragraph below, for example, it takes a reader too long to realize that the topic sentence leads into two arguments supporting its point:

Original:

In the circumstances of this case, imposition of such liability upon Zallea is unwarranted. In this case, there simply were no general standards of steam quality—that is, of the permissible levels of chemicals or corrodents—upon which Zallea reasonably could have relied. The evidence does not support the conclusion that Zallea did have or should have had knowledge of the likelihood of the joint failures sufficient to justify imposing liability upon Zallea. The evidence instead supports a finding that WEPCO was in a position to have superior knowledge of the actual quality and contents of its steam, and to have expertise and access to knowledge concerning the steam in its pipes. Since there were no general industry standards for levels of chemicals or corrodents in light of which Zallea could have designed the expansion joints or issued warnings, and since WEPCO was in a better position to evaluate its own steam quality and chemical or corrodent levels, the loss of the still unexplained failures must fall upon WEPCO rather than Zallea.

A simple road map would have helped:

Revision:

In the circumstances of this case, imposition of such liability upon Zallea is unwarranted for two reasons. First, in this case there simply were no general standards. . . . Second, the evidence supports the conclusion that WEPCO, not Zallea, was in a better position . . . .

❖   **Paragraph Technique 1 B**   ❖

*Develop a paragraph's content in an order
that builds from "old" to "new" information.*

Once you have set an adequate foundation in the opening sentence, take care to link each piece of new or unfamiliar information to what precedes it. As you do this, make the link work cognitively as well as logically: Bring the logic to the surface of your prose so that the reader sees it easily.

Coherent paragraphs can follow many patterns, but in expository paragraphs two simple ones are most common: the topic chain and the topic core. In the first, the language of each sentence refers back to the preceding sentence. In the second, it refers back to a topic announced at the paragraph's start.

The topic chain:

A ⟶ B ⟶ C ⟶ D

The topic core:

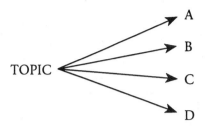

Neither of these patterns is sacred, and the two are often mixed in the same paragraph. Nevertheless, they offer simple reference points from which to analyze a paragraph's shape. This analysis, in turn, will help you make the paragraph's pattern clearer to your readers. In each of the following examples, between the original and revised paragraphs there is only one difference: Some of the sentences have been rewritten to begin with words that show how they fit into the paragraph's pattern. To make these changes, of course, the writer (or editor) first has to see the pattern—or, if the paragraph lacks a clear pattern, to impose one on it.

(1) the *"topic chain"*:

In the example below, the only difference between the two versions is that the second reverses the information in the middle sentence, making the "chain" easier to follow:

Original:

Smith finally received the settlement award in October, 1985. Several months of negotiations led to the release of the funds. But the length of the talks did not reduce the joy of the newly wealthy man or his attorneys.

Revision:

Smith finally received the settlement award in October, 1985. The funds were released only after several months of negotiations. But the length of the talks did not reduce the joy of the newly wealthy man or his attorneys.

(2) the *"topic core"*:

In the next example, the central topic is Dr. Jones' testimony. In the revision, each sentence will start out from that core.

Original:

Under questioning, Dr. Jones testified that Smith had been merely simulating the symptoms of neck injuries, and in fact presented no observable trauma that could explain the pains of which he complained. However, Dr. Jones often treated patients who complained of precisely the same symptoms but who also presented no visible trauma, as he was forced to acknowledge. Therefore, the issue of whether Smith suffered an injury cannot be held to be resolved by Dr. Jones' testimony.

Revision:

Under questioning, Dr. Jones testified that Smith had been merely simulating the symptoms of neck injuries, and in fact presented no observable trauma that could explain the pains of which he complained. However, Dr. Jones was forced to acknowledge that he often treated patients who complained of precisely the same symptoms but who also presented no visible trauma. Therefore, Dr. Jones' testimony cannot be held to resolve the issue of whether Smith . . .

These examples reflect much more than a logical sequence of information. They also illustrate the importance of *where* the logical connections are made within the sentences and *how* they are expressed—in other words, the importance of transitions between sentences. We will return to the art of transitions later in this chapter, where it will serve as a transition of our own into the next chapter on sentence structure.

❖   **PARAGRAPH PRINCIPLE 2**   ❖

At or near its beginning, a paragraph should make clear its significance to the document's analysis.

An introduction should do more than unite the ideas within the paragraph. It should also serve a larger connective purpose by placing the paragraph within the overarching structure of the analysis. This link can be to the basic point of the whole document or of the section, or more modestly to the preceding paragraph. It can be stated explicitly in its own sentence or clause, or it can be implicit in the statement of the paragraph's point.

If the introduction serves this external function well, it also generates another potential benefit. For the reader who is in a hurry and must skim a document for some sense of its essential message, reading only the introductions of each paragraph will provide that kind of summary. In fact, this exercise can be a useful technique for reviewing and tightening your organization from draft to draft.

We turn now to "good" paragraphs. As we noted earlier, a paragraph can be focused and coherent and still no better than adequate. To make it good, you must give it some other qualities.

❖ PARAGRAPH PRINCIPLE 3 ❖

A good paragraph is dynamic as well as coherent: It moves the analysis forward.

The good paragraph propels the reader ahead: Out of its opening point, it develops a consequence that was not entirely predictable. As a result, the reader feels that the paragraph has pushed the analysis onward, rather than simply piling up detail in the same place. For example:

> If Flatlaw were a place, it would be where the vast majority of lawyers, and most law professors, have lived and worked for their entire professional lives. It would be the community law students are trained to join, most of them believing that to dwell there is an attorney's highest professional aspiration. It would probably be where you are now as you read this. This is not to say you should be ashamed, for Flatlaw is not an easy place to reach. But it is an even harder place to leave behind. This article, then, while initially about Flatlaw itself—what it is, where it is, how to get there, and why it is important—also contemplates the meaning and legal significance of moving beyond it. As a consequence, the article is about much more than just law.

By the time we reach the end of this paragraph, although there have been no abrupt lurches forward, we are on new ground. Out of one point, another has emerged.

While there is no formula for organizing a paragraph so that it has this dynamism, the example demonstrates one of the most common patterns: a movement from one point to a contrasting one. Another useful pattern works like a funnel, narrowing the reader's attention from a general topic to the specific point that the writer wants to emphasize:

> This case is not so much a contest between the United States Department of Justice and the two defendant companies as a skirmish in a broader battle over the future direction of American economic life.

> At the center of this struggle is the concept of the conglomerate corporation—not a particularly new development, but one which lately has gained great momentum. One reason for its recent popularity is the attempt of companies to expand by acquiring other firms, while avoiding the antitrust problems of vertical or horizontal mergers. The resulting corporations have none of the earmarks of the traditional trust situation, but they present new problems of their own. Although the market shares of the several component firms within their individual markets remain unchanged in conglomerate mergers, their capital resources become pooled—concentrated into ever fewer hands. Economic concentration is economic power, and the Government is concerned that this trend, if left unchecked, will pose new hazards to the already much-battered competitive system in the United States.

Here, the next-to-last sentence focuses on the crucial fact, the concentration of capital resources—a fact that a less artful writer might instead have put into the opening sentence. The last sentence then phrases this fact as a more specific issue than the paragraph has yet formulated. (It does so, though, with a rhetorical flourish that would be effective only in some contexts.)

In both of these examples, the forward movement arises from the basic structure of the paragraph's thought, although less skillful writers might not have organized the paragraphs to emphasize that dynamism. It is also possible, however, to give a push to paragraphs that are primarily designed to pile detail around one point and, therefore, are basically static. In these cases, the trick is in the content and phrasing of the last sentence. At times, in a version of the "funnel" pattern described above, the writer can divide what would otherwise be a conventional topic sentence into two pieces, the more powerful of which he saves until the paragraph's end:

> The conflict, moreover, involves an important question of law on which a uniform nationwide rule is essential. It would be intolerable, for example, for the minimum wage provisions to have different applications in different regions of the country. Similarly, it would be intolerable for there to exist in some states, but not in others, a judge-made exception to the priority of a secured creditor's perfected lien under the UCC. Because creditors would be reluctant to finance businesses in regions where their liens may not enjoy true priority, the continuing inconsistency on these matters could have serious economic consequences.

At other times, the last sentence, although really no more than a summary of what precedes it, can be phrased so that it opens a new perspective or, at least, adds a new emphasis:

The district court relied on *Henkel v. U.S.*, supra, 237 U.S. 43, 35 S. Ct. 536, 59 L.Ed. 831, for its interpretation of the authority conferred by the 1902 Reclamation Act. *Henkel* held that the broad authority conferred by section 7 of the Reclamation Act was intended to permit acquisition by purchase of Indian lands. The action sanctioned in *Henkel* was of an entirely different character than the action involved here. In *Henkel,* the Indians involved received cash compensation and were permitted to select other allotments in lieu of those taken. In short, *Henkel* involved a purchase, specifically authorized by section 7 of the Reclamation Act. Here, in contrast, the Secretary has never declared an intention to purchase, extinguish, or acquire the Tribe's water rights. No compensation was paid or even offered. Indeed, the government takes the position that acquisition was never intended. *Henkel's* broad dicta can have little independent force in this setting.

Most writers would have ended the paragraph with a sentence like this: "We therefore find that *Henkel* cannot govern this case." Here, it is the phrase "*Henkel*'s broad dicta" that makes the difference, because it characterizes *Henkel*'s conclusions in a new way that captures the essence of the court's refusal to follow that decision.

Here is another example. Again, focus on the last sentence.

We believe that the TVA's interpretation of the statute should be given great weight because of its consistency and longevity, and because of the TVA's reliance upon it since at least the early 50's. In 1951 the TVA relied upon its interpretation to construct the Shawnee Power Plant . . . outside the TVA's statutorily defined service area. . . . In 1953 the TVA constructed the Gallatin Power Plant . . . outside the Tennessee River watershed. . . . In 1959 the TVA constructed the Paradise Power Plant . . . outside the Tennessee River watershed. In 1968 the TVA constructed the Cumberland Power Plant . . . outside the Tennessee River watershed. The proposed Hartsville Power Plant, therefore, would be the fifth TVA electric generating plant located adjacent to, but not within, the watershed of the Tennessee River. The TVA has relied on its interpretation to spend several billion dollars to construct power plants outside the Tennessee River watershed over a 28-year period, providing the electricity necessary for the economic growth and prosperity which now characterizes the Tennessee River Valley region.

One warning about giving paragraphs a rhetorical push at their end: In an analysis that is supposed to be neutral, use this technique sparingly, if at all. It can be a powerfully persuasive device, but not all readers will appreciate the marshalling of rhetorical techniques against them. In many contexts, it is better to sound pedestrian than hyperbolic.

More generally, in legal writing not all paragraphs will be—or should be—as dynamic as those above. Static paragraphs will always be a staple of your prose, because you often want to do no more than unfold details straightforwardly. The proportion should vary, however, from one kind of writing to another. It should be highest in writing designed to be explicitly persuasive, such as briefs, and lowest in strictly expository writing, such as internal research memoranda. Even in the former, good writers will choose the occasions for their most powerful paragraphs carefully.

❖   **PARAGRAPH PRINCIPLE 4**   ❖

A good paragraph anticipates a reader's questions.

Throughout this book, we have emphasized that a writer should understand, and serve, the mental activity that constitutes reading, rather than expecting the reader to be a passive receptacle of the writer's wisdom. This advice applies particularly to paragraphs that assert a point with which disagreement is possible. Most writers would like to assume that, after the paragraph's first sentence, the reader is thinking, "I see. Tell me more." The reader is more likely thinking: "Oh yeah? Says who? Prove it."

In organizing a paragraph, therefore, a skillful writer will not rest content with the patterns of formal logic (syllogisms, induction, and the like). These assume that a reader will be captured by a logical structure that leaves him no choice but to agree with the conclusion. In legal argument, however, a conclusion is seldom so firm. If it persuades, it is usually because the balance falls on its side, not because it is mathematically certain. As you, the writer, load your side of the scales, the reader is engaging you skeptically in a silent debate. Good writers are adept at organizing paragraphs so that they dispose of the reader's questions before he has fully articulated them.

To do this, the most useful model we have found is one proposed by the logician Stephen Toulmin. Although he did not explicitly describe it as a response to a reader's questioning, it arises from a concern with the kinds of support that a reader will accept for a proposition, rather than from traditional logic's concern with the proposition's certainty. In Toulmin's pattern, a claim or conclusion should receive two primary kinds of support: from data or evidence and from a justificatory principle (which he calls a "warrant"). For example:

> (1) Because of the number of parties before the court and the number of dispositive procedural motions now pending, (2) we believe the court should stay discovery pending the entry of a discovery plan, (3) as it is empowered to do by Rules 16 and 26(f) of the Federal Rules of Civil Procedure. (4) As many courts have recognized, "the key to avoiding excessive costs and delay is early and stringent judicial management of the case."

The numbers indicate the following parts of the argument:

(1) factual data supporting the claim,

(2) claim,

(3) legal data supporting the claim, and

(4) warrant or principle supporting the claim (in this case, the principle underlying the legal data).

In addition, many claims are backed by other kinds of support that do not rise to the level of hard, provable data. For example, the paragraph above might continue with this sentence, which points to the consequences of failing to stay discovery:

> Without such management, this case is likely to degenerate into chaos, with the parties taking discovery in inconsistent and duplicative ways.

Finally, a claim's persuasiveness often depends upon the skill with which it is qualified or limited:

> At the moment, only discovery on the jurisdictional issues should be allowed to proceed, since these issues involve a limited number of parties and cannot be rendered moot by the court's decisions on the motions before it.

Toulmin's pattern, instead of striving for certainty, responds to the kinds of objections we might raise if we were asked to do something we did not much want to do. In the paragraph we have been looking at, the writer is responding to these questions:

1. Factual data and claim: "All right, what is the problem here?"

2. Legal data: "Do I really have the authority to do this?"

3. Warrant: "If I do this, am I going to be on the side of right and justice?"

4. Consequences: "Couldn't we really get by without this, even if it's not a bad idea?"

5. Limitation: "Isn't there anything to be said on the other side?"

This model is infinitely flexible. Often, the response to a reader's skepticism need not be as elaborate as in the paragraph above. In this example, focus on the last sentence:

> As to petitioner's claim that his counsel was incompetent and that he was denied effective representation at the trial, there is no evidence to support the charge. This conclusory allegation, so freely made, is amply contradicted by the record. A reading of the trial minutes demonstrates that petitioner's counsel, despite the paucity of defense material, conducted an extremely adequate and resourceful defense, effectively cross-examined prosecution witnesses, particularly the complainant, and made a reasoned plea to the jury in urging acquittal on a reasonable doubt basis. That the jury was not persuaded by his argument, particularly in a case where powerful evidence supports its verdict, by no means furnishes a basis for attacking the competence of counsel.

The last sentence is a canny piece of argumentation. If the paragraph had closed with the penultimate sentence, the instinct of many readers would have been to demur: "If the lawyer was so good, why did he lose?" The last sentence brings the objection into the open and quickly disposes of it. The rebuttal is particularly effective because the writer laid the ground for it earlier in the paragraph, by referring to the weakness of the defense's case.

❖ **PARAGRAPH PRINCIPLE 5** ❖

A good paragraph makes use of natural points of emphasis.

As we said in Chapter 1, readers are not computers. They do not perceive written information as equal bits of data to be stored carefully until they are told how to use them. Instead, readers gather and retain data with a subliminal sense of their limitations: They sift, assess, and make quick choices about what to remember and what to let pass (perhaps for later review). This observation is at the heart of the distinction between cognitive and logical organization, and it leads us here to a new question: How can a writer take advantage of a reader's instinctive mental activity to emphasize important information?

One technique, of course, is simply to change typeface—to bold, italics, or underlining—so as to catch the reader's eye the way voice inflection would catch his ear. This works, but only to a point. Readers confronted with frequent or lengthy changes in typeface will simply tune them out and, indeed, become annoyed with them. A much better alternative involves subtlety rather than shouting: Organize your information so that the reader provides the emphasis himself.

To demonstrate this idea, imagine a series of random numbers read aloud to an audience—4, 11, 3, 47, 25, and so on. Experiments reveal that if the audience is asked the first number, a sizable majority can recall it; and if asked the last number, even more remember it; but if asked the middle numbers, almost no one can identify them. The lesson is simple: Our minds give a natural emphasis to the beginning and end of any sequence, with slightly more emphasis falling on the end. And, correspondingly, we deemphasize the information in the middle.

A paragraph, of course, is a flow or sequence of information, and applying this principle to it yields the following techniques:

❖ **Paragraph Technique 5A** ❖

Put key information at the beginning and end of the paragraph.

This point was implicit in much of what we have been saying about organizing paragraphs. Pay particular attention both to the opening of a paragraph and to its closing punch line. Consider the following example, drawn from an article about legal reasoning. The word "logic" forms the link with the preceding paragraph:

> Our logic is surrounded by a wall of paradox. Inside this boundary, logic resolves informational conflicts to our satisfaction; outside, it does not, leaving contradictions and absurdities. The difference seems to be between sense and nonsense, between logic and illogic. But perhaps this dichotomy is a bit too stark. Perhaps there exists another category between, on the one hand, those phenomena we happily accept because they can be explained by our logic and, on the other, those we comfortably reject because they are in direct conflict with logic. We would arrive at this remarkable middle category, then, by opening our minds to phenomena logic cannot explain. I will call this nonlogical mental process "faith."

But what should you do, you might ask, if your paragraph has a key point unavoidably located in its middle? Two techniques are available:

> ❖ **Paragraph Technique 5 B** ❖
>
> *To emphasize information within a paragraph, structure your sentences to make readers pause over what is important.*

> ❖ **Paragraph Technique 5C** ❖
>
> *To give especially strong emphasis to an interior point, put it into a short sentence surrounded by longer ones.*

Here is Winston Churchill at work with both techniques, in a passage from his *History of the Second World War*:

> We must take September 15 as the culminating date. On this date the Luftwaffe, after two heavy attacks on the 14th, made its greatest concentrated effort in a resumed attack on London. It was one of the decisive battles of the war, and, like the Battle of Waterloo, it was on a Sunday. I was at Chequers. I had already on several occasions visited the headquarters of Number 11 Fighter Group in order to witness the conduct of an air battle, when not much happened. However, the weather on this day seemed suitable to the enemy and accordingly I drove over to Uxbridge and arrived at the Group Headquarters . . . .

Note how the second sentence forces us to slow down by inserting a phrase between its subject and verb, and how the third sentence also cannot be read too quickly. The effect is to emphasize the words over which the sentences' structure makes us pause. Then note how the brevity of the next sentence stands out by contrast. We might quarrel with Churchill's choice of what to emphasize in this sentence: As the war rages around him, he takes the crucial fact to be where he was when the battle began. But the technique is masterful.

Finally, Churchill uses one more technique for the sake of emphasis. Although this quoted passage appears above as one paragraph, Churchill wrote it as two:

We must take September 15 as the culminating date. On this date the Luftwaffe, after two heavy attacks on the 14th, made its greatest concentrated effort in a resumed attack on London.

It was one of the decisive battles of the war, and . . . .

This paragraphing has nothing to do with logic: It exists solely to interrupt the passage's flow, and thus to add even more emphasis to the second and third sentences.*

❖   **PARAGRAPH PRINCIPLE 6**   ❖

A good paragraph provides smooth transitions among its sentences.

We return to the topic we raised on page 4–6. On the assumption that your sentences form a logical sequence, let's turn again to cognitive psychology. As we noted near the start of this book, your organizational duties do not end with logic. You must also make it as easy as possible for readers to perceive the structure of your reasoning. This admonition applies as much to a paragraph as to the entire document. In a paragraph, it is not enough to get the sentences in the right sequence. You must also get the words of each sentence into an order that makes it easy for readers to see, as they move from one sentence to the next, how the sentences connect. Readers will begin to look for this connection at the start of the new sentence and, until they find it, they will be reading in a state of subliminal anxiety that will prevent them from concentrating sharply on the sentence's details.

The secret to writing paragraphs in which one sentence flows smoothly into the next, then, is to follow the "old info → new info" pattern. Sentences should begin with familiar information, or with a clear reference to it, or with a clear signal of what you are going to do with it (add to it, qualify it, contradict it, etc.). In the example below, which we used a few pages ago for a different purpose, both the original and revised paragraphs contain the same information in the same sequence of sentences, but the revision rearranges the infor-

---

* In *Style: An Anti-Textbook* (1974), where we found this passage, Richard A. Lanham uses it to demonstrate a different but closely related point: Churchill as a writer retains an orator's skill in the manipulation of stress and pitch.

mation within the two middle sentences to ensure that each sentence leads comfortably into the next.

Original:

This case is not so much a contest between the United States Department of Justice and the two defendant companies as a skirmish in a broader battle over the future direction of American economic life. The concept of the conglomerate corporation—not a particularly new development, but one which lately has gained great momentum—is at the center of this struggle. The attempt of companies to expand by acquiring other firms, while avoiding the antitrust problems of vertical or horizontal mergers, is one reason for the recent popularity of this concept. The resulting corporations have none of the earmarks of the traditional trust situation, but they present new problems of their own.

Revision:

This case is not so much a contest between the United States Department of Justice and the two defendant companies as a skirmish in a broader battle over the future direction of American economic life. At the center of this struggle is the concept of the conglomerate corporation—not a particularly new development, but one which lately has gained great momentum. One reason for its recent popularity is the attempt of companies to expand by acquiring other firms, while avoiding the antitrust problems of vertical or horizontal mergers. The resulting corporations have none of the earmarks of the traditional trust situation, but they present new problems of their own.

Here is a more complicated example, with the revision's transitions italicized:

Original:

Governmental immunity is the doctrine under which the sovereign, be it country, state, county or municipality, may not be sued without its consent. [citation] The purpose of the immunity of public officials is not directly to protect the sovereign, but to protect the public official while he performs his governmental function, and it is thus a more limited immunity than governmental immunity. Courts have generally extended less than absolute immunity for that reason. The distinction between discretionary acts and ministerial acts is the most commonly recognized distinction. The official is immune only when what he does while performing his lawful duties requires "personal deliberation, decision, and judgment." [citation]

Revision:

Governmental immunity is the doctrine under which the sovereign, be it country, state, county or municipality, may not be sued without its consent. [citation] The *immunity* of public officials, *on the other hand*, is a more limited principle, since its purpose is not directly to protect the sovereign, but to protect the public official while he performs his governmental function. *Because of the principle's more limited scope*, courts have generally extended less than absolute immunity to public officials. *The most commonly recognized limitation* arises from the distinction between discretionary and ministerial acts. *Under this distinction*, the official is immune only when what he does while performing his lawful duties requires "personal deliberation, decision, and judgment." [citation]

Although this principle of using transitions is easy to grasp, it can be hard to apply for psychological rather than technical reasons. As a writer starts a new sentence, his attention is naturally turned to new content. Though he will (he devoutly hopes) know when he starts the sentence how it connects with the previous one, his instinct may well be to get the new information down first, before he loses it, and then worry about the connections. If he does this habitually, however, he has not yet learned—as all professional writers must—to put his readers' needs before his own.

A writer can create smoother transitions through four techniques.

❖ **Paragraph Technique 6A** ❖

At or near the beginning of a sentence, repeat part of the preceding sentence's content, using the same words or easily recognizable synonyms or allusions.

For example:

The statute clearly *requires* enforcement of the completed note unless it is proved that the completion was unauthorized. In effect, *this requirement* creates . . .

To use this technique, it is often enough to rearrange a sentence so that the connecting words move from its end to its beginning:

Original:

The award of child support and maintenance are within the discretion of the trial court, and its decision will not be disturbed unless it has *abused* that discretion. A failure to consider relevant factors is an *abuse* of discretion.

Revision:

The award of child support and maintenance are within the discretion of the trial court, and its decision will not be disturbed unless it has *abused* that discretion. An *abuse* occurs when it fails to consider relevant factors.

The repetition does not have to be as explicit as it is in these examples. In the next example, seen before in another context, the writer relies instead on rephrasings:

As to petitioner's claim that his counsel was incompetent and that he was denied effective representation at the trial, there is no evidence to support *the charge. This conclusory allegation,* so freely made, is amply contradicted by *the record.* A reading of *the trial minutes* demonstrates that . . .

In the final example, the content of the linking words is enough to create the transition:

Original:

The plaintiff was a mortgage lender to the two debtors. Three parcels of real estate comprised the plaintiff's collateral, which secured the note or mortgage.

Revision:

The plaintiff was a mortgage lender to the two debtors. Its note and mortgage were secured by collateral consisting of three parcels of real estate.

But do not steer away from simple repetition because you fear it is unsophisticated and dull. In prose that is meant to be absorbed as quickly as the complexity of its content allows, some repetition is helpful. Like the repetition of words on highway signs, it keeps us on track, and reassured, in the middle of complicated maneuvering.

❖ **Paragraph Technique 6B** ❖

At or near the beginning of a sentence, use a word or phrase that shows the sentence's logical connection to the previous one: Does it qualify it? Add to it? Rephrase its point?

Our language is rich in these connecting devices ("however," "similarly," "in contrast," "also," "nevertheless"). Because they are easier to use than the other techniques we describe, some writers use them too much, in an effort to patch together a shaky sequence of sentences. Be aware of this danger, but also remember how useful these words can be for prose designed to be understood quickly and clearly.[*]

Here is a paragraph that, like the paragraph about immunity, uses both methods to link its sentences:

> As in *Fleming*, the proposed conditions on Smith's continued practice of law appear reasonably directed to his rehabilitation from alcoholism. Unlike the situation in *Fleming*, however, Smith has previously had his license suspended for unprofessional conduct. Further, Smith violated one of the conditions imposed upon him by the Court when he resumed the use of alcohol. Consequently, we do not consider that the continued imposition of conditions on Smith's practice is sufficient response to his conduct. Rather, it is appropriate that Smith's license be suspended for 30 days, following which the conditions to which he stipulated be imposed on his continued practice.

One qualification to these two techniques before we go on to two others: Do not overuse them. The transitions do not always need to occupy the very first words in the sentence. Nor, in fact, does every sentence need an explicit transition. Readers are smart enough to make some connections themselves. If you seem to be underlining the obvious, you will irritate them.

---

[*] You may have been taught, incidentally, not to start sentences with "and," "but," "however," and the like, the purported rule being that these words should connect only clauses within a sentence. That notion always had more pedantry than common sense behind it, and it is now usefully ignored by most professional writers. Whether you should ignore it depends upon your audience. If it is conservative, you may not want to wave stylistic red flags in front of it.

> ❖ **Paragraph Technique 6C** ❖
>
> *At the beginning of each sentence, show how the sentence fits into the paragraph's overall pattern.*

For example, if you are describing a set of facts whose temporal relationship is important, begin each sentence by stating when the action it describes happened: "On March 5 . . . ," "Two weeks later . . . ," "At about the same time . . . ." Or, if you are showing that someone was negligent in several ways, begin each sentence by repeating his negligence: "Defendant failed to . . . ," "Nor did he point out that . . ." "And he had not taken the precaution of . . . ."

> ❖ **Paragraph Technique 6D** ❖
>
> *Occasionally, use an entire sentence as a road sign (as opposed to the larger "road map" discussed earlier) to show the reader what lies ahead.*

This technique is seldom necessary in short paragraphs, but in longer ones it is a handy device in three situations: when you turn from one subtopic to another, when you are about to present a list, and when you introduce a long quotation. In these situations, sentences like the following will help even though they seem to state the obvious:

We now turn to the second issue.

To resolve this issue, we must answer the following three questions.

As the following quotation shows, *Wigmore* contradicts the plaintiff's contention.

To sum up this principle, here is a final example. Many of the examples above were chosen to make a point, and they may have seemed a little exaggerated. This is a more restrained example of the skillful use of transitions. Notice how each sentence begins with a word or phrase that quickly and unobtrusively connects it with the previous sentence.

The merger price of $52.50 complies fully with Delaware law requiring a company to offer a fair price to stockholders in effecting a merger. *Weinberger v. U.O.P.* established the standard for determining fairness of price, eliminating exclusive reliance on the Delaware Block Method and its weighted average of asset value, market price, and earnings. In its place, the Delaware Supreme Court adopted a "more liberal approach," under which a court must consider "proof of value by any techniques or methods which are generally considered acceptable in the financial community and otherwise admissible in court." 457 A. 2d at 713. Such an evaluation must include "all relevant factors: assets, market value, earnings, future prospects, and any other elements that affect the intrinsic or inherent value of a company's stock." *Id.* at 711.

In considering these factors, the goal is to ascertain the inherent value of the company, in order to pay the stockholder his proportionate interest in the stock which has been taken by the merger. *Id.* at 713. However, "the stockholder is only entitled to be paid for that which has been taken from him . . . [that is,] his proportionate interest in a going concern." *Id.* The stockholder is not entitled to any elements of future value which are not known or susceptible of proof as of the date of the merger . . . .

❖   **PARAGRAPH PRINCIPLE 7**   ❖

A good paragraph has variety in the length and rhythm of its sentences.

When we read legal prose, we are usually conscious only of the meaning it conveys. Yet it also affects us by its rhythm, even if we are not aware of the effect. Monotony dulls our attention to what we are reading; variety keeps us alert and interested. We will return to this principle in detail in the next chapter on sentences and in Chapter 8 on style.

CHAPTER **5**

Writing Sentences:
The Wages of Syntax

MANY UNPRACTICED WRITERS believe that the mark of a good style is the impressiveness of its vocabulary. But a glance at the prose in magazines such as *Atlantic* or *Harper's* or *Sports Illustrated*—or in the opinions of Justice Holmes—shows otherwise. What truly distinguishes professional writers is their control over syntax, their ability to construct sentences in more ways than the amateur can, and to shape each to suit its purpose.

This control is important for several reasons. It allows you to vary the rhythm of a paragraph. It allows you to apply at the level of the sentence your concern for organizing to help the reader perceive your logic. It allows you to write longer sentences that are easy to read, something that takes a good deal of skill. And it allows you to control nuances of meaning, because meaning arises not just from the words that state a fact or idea, but from the syntax into which those words are combined. Sentence structure, then, is not just a matter of "style," of dressing up the prose to make it look more attractive. It affects both content and the reader's ability to absorb and remember that content.

This means that it is not enough to follow the rules of grammar. A grammatically correct sentence is not necessarily a well-written one. The larger issue is how you control syntax to make it serve the ends of clarity and precision.

The principles below point the way to strong, clear, persuasive sentences. You may wonder, however, about why some familiar advice is not in our list: We will not tell you, for example, to make sure pronouns have clear referents, or to keep related words together, or to express parallel ideas in parallel grammatical form, or to avoid dangling participles. We will not even emphasize the common admonition to write short sentences. We assume you have assimilated all this advice, even if you slip up occasionally. (Strunk and White's *The Elements of Style* provides pointed reminders, and at the end of this Chapter we will warn about situations that often cause trouble even for good writers.) Instead, we will emphasize principles and techniques that your education is less likely to have driven home, and that are particularly important when you write about complicated subjects.

To help organize this advice, bear in mind that sentences fall into two broad categories: sentences about action, and sentences about concepts or states of mind. Some of these principles and techniques pertain to both categories, some only to the first.

❖ **SENTENCE PRINCIPLE 1** ❖

A sentence will be clearest if its grammatical core—subject, verb, and object—contains the core of its content.

This principle, like most of those this book describes, arises from an understanding of the mental activity of reading. To digest a sentence, a reader must do two things simultaneously: decipher its grammatical structure and grasp its content. The grammar rests upon a familiar core: (1) the subject of the sentence, (2) the verb, and (sometimes) (3) the object of the verb. If the reader can find the substantive core of the sentence in the same place—that is, in the same words—as the grammatical core, then he will have to do less work to read the sentence and is more likely to remember its content. Consider the following two examples:

Original:

The factor that persuaded the judge to grant the motion was the expert's report.

Revision:

The expert's report persuaded the judge to grant the motion.

Original:

The reason for there having been less utilization by corporations of funded programs than unfunded programs is the following . . . .

Revision:

Corporations have used funded programs less often than unfunded programs because . . . .

In the originals, the subjects ("factor" and "reason") and the verbs ("was" and "is") tell us nothing worth knowing about the sentences' content. In the revisions, they provide much of the meat of the sentences, and the objects provide most of the rest.

This basic principle—match grammar and content—can be implemented through three techniques.

❖ **Sentence Technique 1A** ❖

Make the grammatical subject the key topic of the sentence.

The *grammatical* subject of a sentence may not, of course, be its *conceptual* subject or topic. For example:

Original:

The instance of the plaintiff's weeping on the stand did not seem to affect the jury.

The grammatical subject here is "instance"; the topic is "plaintiff's weeping." A simple revision matches subject and topic:

Revision:

Plaintiff's weeping on the stand did not seem to affect the jury.

The problem is easy to spot when the subject has no real content. It may be harder to spot when the subject has content, but the wrong content. For example:

Original:

The court found that implementing the proposal would require defendant to breach existing contracts.

If the focus should be on the court, then the writer has chosen the right main subject and verb ("court"/"found"). If the focus should instead be on the defendant's unhappy situation, then the sentence needs to be reorganized.

> *Revision:*
>
> Defendant would have to breach existing contracts to implement the proposal, the court found.
>
> *or*
>
> To implement the proposal, the court found, defendant would have to breach existing contracts.

For sentences that describe action, this technique takes the following form.

❖　　**Sentence Technique 1B**　　❖

In a sentence that describes action, make the grammatical subject the agent or "doer" of the action, make the verb the action, and make the object the goal of the action.

When we were young, before education complicated matters, we had no trouble applying this technique. When you came home from a tough day in the schoolyard, you would say something like this:

> Johnny tried to steal my marbles, Mama.

Once you reach law school, however, there is a good chance that the facts in a marble-stealing case will come out something like this:

> An attempt was made by Johnny at the theft of Sam's marbles.

The act almost disappears under the verbiage. To make an act stand out in a sentence, organize it to match the diagram below—as you once did instinctively, without needing a diagram:

subject	verb	object
agent	action	goal

This advice applies not only to a sentence, but also to clauses within a sentence. For example:

Original:

In *Channel*, the court addressed the defendant's representations that its supply and productive capacity for a certain product was such as rendered it capable of selling to the plaintiff a certain quantity each month.

The sentence's main subject, verb, and object are fine, but the next clause is a disaster.

Revision:

In *Channel*, the court addressed the defendant's representations that it could produce and supply enough of a product to sell the plaintiff a certain quantity each month.

Here is another, more complex example:

Original:

Failure to produce the relevant documents on time delayed our realization of the issue's importance until deposition scheduling was complete.

This example is tricky because the sentence describes several actions and at least two agents ("we" and whoever failed). All of this activity is packed tightly into a small space. To apply the technique, first unpack the sentence's contents, and then devote a separate clause to each action.

Revision:

Because plaintiff failed to produce the documents on time, we did not realize the issue's importance until we had already scheduled depositions.

This technique, therefore, has a corollary: In general, do not describe more than one action in a clause.

When you apply this technique, you will occasionally need to think twice about your choice of an agent. With the sentence below, for instance, you might decide to throw the emphasis on either the banks or the depositors:

Original:

The primary motivation for United States depositors to place their funds with a branch outside the United States is to receive a higher rate of return.

Revision 1:

United States depositors place their funds with a branch outside the United States primarily because they want to receive a higher rate of return.

Revision 2:

Branches outside the United States attract funds from United States depositors primarily because they pay a higher rate of return.

This technique is particularly useful for litigators when they want to emphasize the sins of their opponents:

Original:

Even if the alleged contracts were enforceable, plaintiffs' failure to sell a single national advertisement resulted in a breach of the alleged contracts.

Revision:

Even if the alleged contracts were enforceable, plaintiffs breached them by failing to sell a single national advertisement.

The revision not only puts action into the verb ("breached" rather than "resulted in"), it ties that action directly to the plaintiffs ("plaintiffs breached"). It thus associates the plaintiffs with an action that is legally relevant—"breached"—rather than an abstract event—"failure to sell."

A third technique expands upon the first two:

> ❖ **Sentence Technique 1C** ❖
>
> *Keep the subject close to the verb and the verb close to the object. In other words, keep the grammatical core of the sentence intact.*

Readers, particularly when they are dealing with a complex document, read in a subliminal state of anxiety. They do not want to be tantalized by a sentence: They want its central thought to be handed to them neatly and clearly. A complete thought generally requires a subject and a verb and sometimes an object ("He threw *the ball*.") or a complement ("The ball is *red*."). Hence, as soon as readers see a sentence's grammatical subject, they start to look for the accompanying verb; and once they see the verb, if it demands an object or complement they are unfulfilled until they find one.

Consider the following example:

Original:

A *number of nations* in response to what they thought to be an inappropriate extraterritorial investigation by the United States *enacted blocking statutes* intended to frustrate the investigation.

The correction is simple: Remove the parenthetical phrase from between the subject and verb.

Revision:

In response to what they thought to be an inappropriate extraterritorial investigation by the United States, a *number of nations enacted blocking statutes* intended to frustrate the investigation.

When this cure does not work, you will need to rebuild the sentence more fundamentally, usually by breaking it into more than one clause:

Original:

Thus, an interpretation that the proof of disability could be given at any time while the insured was still living would require ignoring clear and repeated language in the rider regarding the termination of the right to claim waiver of premium.

Revision:

Thus, to conclude that proof of disability could be given at any time while the insured was alive, this Court would have to ignore the rider's clear and repeated language about the termination of the right to claim waiver of premium.

This technique is far from an absolute commandment, however. A two- or three-word phrase between two of a sentence's main parts will not usually bother a reader. And, if the sentence's grammatical subject is its first word, most readers are undisturbed by a fairly long phrase between it and the verb, perhaps because this kind of sentence is so much a favorite of journalists that we have become habituated to it. In addition, as we discuss on page 5–19, a skillful writer will sometimes go out of his way to insert an interrupting phrase in order to make the rhythm of a sentence more compelling, or to emphasize a point.

So far, we have simply assumed that sentences either describe actions or do not. In practice, however, many writers tend to push sentences from the first category into the second: That is, they do their best to disguise the action to which a sentence refers. This sometimes happens because, by hiding the activity, a writer also hides responsibility and, perhaps, avoids blame. But it also happens because some writers have an unarticulated feeling that actions are a little crude, and best covered with some conceptual finery. This feeling, if unchecked, has disastrous effects.

❖   **SENTENCE PRINCIPLE 2**   ❖

A sentence will be more forceful and more memorable if it describes actions rather than concepts or states of mind.

The second principle, like the first, arises from an understanding of how readers absorb information. However sophisticated our educations, we still find it easier to grasp and remember an action than, say, a definition. This should come as no surprise to anyone who has gone through law school. It is one reason for the case method of instruction: stories of litigated conflicts, of actions by the parties and the courts, teach the legal doctrines involved more vividly and memorably.

In other words, our readers would rather be told a story. As a result, the more clearly a sentence describes action, the stronger its impact. Some examples:

EXAMPLE 1

Original:

An argument for the exposure approach has the benefit of utilizing the principle that ambiguous language should be construed to promote coverage.

Revision:

If we argue for the exposure approach, we can then rely on the principle that ambiguous language should be construed to promote coverage.

EXAMPLE 2

Original:

Compensation for the California damage claimants remains a significant public policy concern counseling application of California law in a California forum.

Revision 1:

If California damage claimants are to receive adequate compensation, as public policy dictates they should, then the courts must require that California law be applied in a California forum.

Revision 2:

Public policy dictates that California damage claimants should receive adequate compensation. To ensure this result, the courts must require that California law be applied in a California forum.

Note one aspect of both revisions. They not only throw more emphasis on the damage claimants and the courts, the chief players in this drama, but they also turn "public policy," an amorphous concept, into an actor by hooking it to a strong verb. This technique can do wonders to bring life to what would otherwise be a dry passage. Here is Justice Jackson describing the purpose of a statute dealing with shareholder litigation:

> Equity came to the relief of the stockholder, who had no standing to bring civil action at law against faithless directors and managers. Equity, however, allowed him to step into the corporation's shoes and to seek in its right the restitution he could not demand in his own. It required him first to demand that the corporation vindicate its own rights, but when, as was usual, those who perpetrated the

wrongs also were able to obstruct any remedy, equity would hear and adjudge the corporation's cause through its stockholder. . . .

Cohen v. Beneficial Industrial Loan Corp., 337 U.S. 541, 548 (1949).

We do not want to overstate the scope of this principle, however. Particularly in legal writing, you often need to write about concepts rather than actions, and to write about them as elements in an analysis rather than—as Jackson did—as actors in a metaphorical drama. Consider this example:

Original:

As a result of a conspiracy among Megacorp and its creditor banks to delay the filing of Megacorp's bankruptcy petition until the bank's appropriation of the proceeds of Imperial's sale of crude oil, Imperial was deprived of payment for the oil.

Possible Revision:

Because Megacorp and its creditor banks conspired to delay the filing of Megacorp's bankruptcy petition until the banks had appropriated the proceeds from Imperial's sale of the crude oil, Imperial was deprived of payment.

The revision focuses unflinchingly on who did what, while the original throws the emphasis instead on states of affairs (a conspiracy, an appropriation of proceeds). The revision is therefore a stronger and more memorable sentence, and you would probably choose it if you represented Imperial or even if you were a neutral observer. But the original also has its uses. Because it focuses on the conspiracy and appropriation of proceeds, it is the better choice if you are writing about a legal question that turns on the proof of those elements. If this is the case, then even a litigator representing Imperial might find a place for the original version during the course of a brief.

But the basic point remains: If you have a choice between expressing your information in the form of a concept or an action, choose the action.

Sentence Technique 1B above described the most important method for expressing actions clearly (put the actor in the subject, the action in the verb, and so on). Here are three additional techniques that reinforce that lesson.

❖ **Sentence Technique 2A** ❖

Avoid the passive voice.

If a sentence describes an action, then its verb should ordinarily be in the active voice. Simply put, when you use active voice, the subject of the sentence acts and the object of the verb is acted upon:

> The union *filed* a complaint.
>
> An attorney who *receives* a client's funds *must deposit* them into the Client Trust Account.

When you use passive voice, the subject of the sentence is acted upon, and a form of the verb "to be" precedes the verb:

> A complaint *was filed* by the union.
>
> A client's funds that have been received by an attorney *must be deposited* into the Client Trust Account.

Passive voice has two primary disadvantages. First, it blurs the clarity of the action: Objects replace agents and verbs become limp and hollow. Second, it often leads to ambiguity because the agent often disappears from the sentence altogether.

> A complaint was filed [by whom?].
>
> A client's funds must be deposited into the Client Trust Account [by whom?].
>
> The situation was analyzed [by whom?].

However, passive voice does have its place, as we pointed out in Chapter 1:

❖ When the object of the verb (or goal of the action) is more important than the subject. In this situation, the passive allows you to emphasize your topic properly or to follow the "old info → new info" pattern. Consider the example on page 4–6 involving Dr. Jones. In order to maintain the paragraph's organizing pattern, the second and third sentences are both in passive form.

❖ When we do not know the cause or agent, or when it is unimportant. Example: "Traffic was brought to a halt" *or* "Traffic was snarled for two hours."

❖ When the writer wishes to disassociate himself from the statement without actually attributing it to someone else. Example: "Overruns are projected . . ."

❖ When the writer *wants* to be less than clear and direct (for example, in some interrogatory answers).

❖ **Sentence Technique 2B** ❖

Express important actions in verbs, not in nouns and adjectives. In other words, avoid "nominalization."

Although this is common advice, and good advice, we have already suggested why lawyers who so often deal with concepts rather than actions should approach it with care. We will return to this point more fully on page 7–6. For present purposes, the following examples make our point:

Original:

The unit had *performance problems,* primarily as a result of a *lack of* technical knowledge about such mechanisms.

Revision:

The unit *performed badly,* primarily because its members *lacked* technical knowledge about such mechanisms.

Original:

The defendant's *intention* is to implement a *modification* of the program.

Revision:

The defendant *intends* to *modify* the program.

In the original versions, the words that describe the most important actions are italicized. Invariably, they are nouns. The revisions change them into verbs, thus matching form to content.

❖   **Sentence Technique 2C**   ❖

When you state a proposition that denies or contradicts another, choose carefully between a positive form that conveys action and a negative form that suggests inaction.

For example:

Original:

No commission will be payable to X unless . . . .

Revision:

Y will pay a commission to X only if . . . .

Original:

The Court did not adopt the defendant's theory . . . .

Revision:

The Court rejected the defendant's theory . . . .

In the second example, the original is the politer sentence, and it may therefore be the better choice in some circumstances. Unless you are going out of your way to be low-key, however, choose the positive form because it is easier for readers to digest and remember. In a short sentence, the difference may not be great, but it becomes significant in longer, more complicated ones—especially if they contain more than one negative. For example, the multiple negatives that often appear in contracts limiting future contingencies are particularly hard to follow. Here is a truly fine example:

> Notwithstanding the foregoing, the foregoing section shall be deemed to be a covenant of Mortgagor under this Mortgage to pay any federal income taxes due and owing; provided, however, that failure to pay the same does not result in a lien against the Trust Estate or any portion thereof which is not a Permitted Lien as defined in the Company Credit Agreement.

We confess that we do not understand this provision well enough to revise it.

In addition to obvious negative words such as "no," "not," and "never," be cautious in the use, overuse, and unfortunate combination of other negative terms, such as:

❖ negative adjectives (unsupported, unproven)

❖ implicitly negative verbs (exclude, preclude, prohibit, fail)

❖ implicitly negative connecting words (unless, except, without, against).

❖   **SENTENCE PRINCIPLE 3**   ❖

A sentence should be organized to give appropriate emphasis to each piece of information in it.

Consider, for example, the following versions of the same information.

1. Harrigan was the manager of the marina. He testified that the boat was delivered to the marina on January 7, but he didn't see it there again after January 8.
2. Harrigan, the manager of the marina, testified that he last saw the boat on January 8, the day after it was delivered.
3. Harrigan, the manager of the marina, testified that he last saw the boat on January 8. It had been delivered on January 7.

The first version implies that Harrigan's identity, which gets a sentence to itself, is important. It also implies that the date of the boat's arrival and the date of its last sighting are of about the same importance: each gets an independent clause to itself, though some extra emphasis is thrown on the last fact. You can judge for yourself the differences between these emphases and the ones created by the other versions.

The differences here are matters of nuance. As a result, many writers would not consciously choose one sentence structure over another for the sake of emphasis. But this choice is important. As we argued in our section on paragraphs, emphasis is more than rhetorical cosmetics. It conveys meaning. Meaning arises from the relationship of facts, not just from their simple addition, and part of this relationship is a hierarchy of significance.

To control emphasis in a sentence, you have four techniques at your disposal.

❖   **Sentence Technique 3A**   ❖

*In longer sentences, place your most
significant information at the end.*

Just as in a paragraph, the natural points of emphasis in a sentence fall at the beginning and the end, with the end receiving greater stress. In general, then, the crucial information, the piece you want the reader to remember above all else, should come at the end. (The beginning will often be occupied by a transition from the preceding sentence, in line with the "old info → new info" principle.) Inexperienced writers characteristically drop the important information into the sentence wherever it first occurs to them—often at the start, sometimes buried in the middle. Here, as in other stylistic matters, we may have to retrain our mental muscles to accept new habits.[*]

Original:

The employee was instructed to pump the bilge of a boat into the water. He refused to do so after seeing a posted notice stating that such pumping was illegal and after calling the Coast Guard to confirm this fact.

Revision:

The employee was instructed to pump the bilge of a boat into the water. After seeing a posted notice stating that such pumping was illegal and after calling the Coast Guard to confirm this fact, he refused to do so.

---

[*] This technique explains why you should be wary of ending sentences with prepositions. Although it is not a grammatical sin, as most of us were once taught, it wastes the point of maximum emphasis: The sentence ends with a lifeless little word that has no content itself, but merely tags after the sentence's verb. *Original*: ". . . situations we find ourselves in." *Revision*: ". . . situations in which we find ourselves." The revision is not always this easy. At times, simply moving the preposition will produce a stilted sentence, and you will have to look instead for a way of recasting it. Occasionally, a preposition may be the best way to end a sentence—but not often. In formal legal writing, we suggest you never try it, even in the rare cases when it is stylistically justified. Some readers will regard it as a mistake or, more charitably, a colloquialism, and you will not have a chance to argue the verdict.

❖   **Sentence Technique 3B**   ❖

Avoid "throat clearing" at the beginning of a sentence.

"Throat clearing" places a string of unnecessary, empty words at the beginning of the sentence:

It is often said that . . .

It was not long before he . . .

It seems that . . .

It is important to add that . . .

It may be recalled that . . .

It is interesting to point out that . . .

There is . . .

It is not clear that there must be . . .

This structure causes three problems: First, and most obviously, it is verbose. Second, it violates Sentence Principle 1 by wasting the subject and verb of the sentence, and thereby mismatching grammar and content. Third, and of particular relevance here, it wastes the opening of the sentence, the part that receives extra attention from the reader. The cure is sometimes easy:

Original:

There is very little Georgia law which addresses this issue.

Revision:

Very little Georgia law addresses this issue.

At other times, however, the simple fix of excising the opening words does not work. You have to rewrite the sentence to create an effective subject and verb.

Original:

Here, the Debtor listed "inventory" and "intercompany receivables" as assets in the Petition. There was no attempt at that stage, therefore, to conceal the property.

Revision:

Here, the Debtor listed "inventory" and "intercompany receivables" as assets in the Petition. At that stage, therefore, Debtor was not attempting to conceal the property.

When you try this cure, be careful not to replace the "throat clearing" with a syntax that is not much better. For example, in the first revision below, "There is" is replaced by an equally hollow verb ("exists" or "is contained"):

Original:

There is important data in this document.

Revision 1:

Important data exists [or "is contained"] in this document.

To make the sentence stronger, you would need to reorder its information:

Revision 2:

This document contains important data.

Despite these warnings, you may nevertheless sometimes choose a "throat clearing" opening simply because it is common in ordinary speech and is therefore comfortable to a reader. (See the quotations from E.B. White in Appendix B.) But bear in mind that "throat clearing" is common in speech in part because we can compensate for it by using voice inflection to emphasize the more important parts of the sentence.

❖   **Sentence Technique 3C**   ❖

Put your more important information in "larger" grammatical containers and less important information in "smaller" containers.

As the sentences on page 5–14 about Harrigan's marina demonstrated, you can control emphasis through the kind of grammatical container—sentence, clause, phrase, or word—into which you put a piece of information. The concept is simple: the higher the container in the hierarchy of grammatical importance, the more emphasis its content receives. A sentence counts for more than a clause, an independent clause counts for more than a dependent one, and either counts for more than a phrase.

If you are writing as an advocate, this technique of syntactical emphasis can be a powerful tool because it allows you to give the most weight to facts supporting your conclusion. Here are two examples:

EXAMPLE 1

Original:

After her parents' divorce, Joan experienced emotional problems for which her father arranged counseling and therapy. Since therapy began, Joan's problems have decreased. Her counselor at school testified *that she still needs help, but that the proposed move would not harm her if her father found similar services in Alaska.*

Revision:

After her parents' divorce, Joan experienced emotional problems for which her father arranged counseling and therapy. Since therapy began, Joan's problems have decreased. Her counselor at school testified *that, while she still needs help, the proposed move would not harm her if her father found similar services in Alaska.*

EXAMPLE 2

Original:

At trial, the victim, his friends, and the defendant all testified. In several aspects their testimony conflicts, though not significantly.

Revision:

At trial, the victim, his friends, and the defendant all testified. Although their testimony conflicts in several aspects, none of the inconsistencies is significant.

Even when you are not writing as an advocate, use syntax to signal the relative importance of information:

Original:

Before the hearing for summary judgment, appellant's counsel stipulated that he had not served a notice of intent to file litigation against appellees. The trial court heard argument on May 9, 1989, and entered final summary judgment in favor of appellees which in essence was based on the applicability of § 768.57 and appellant's failure to comply with the pre-filing notice requirements of the statute.

Revision:

Before the hearing for summary judgment, appellant's counsel stipulated that he had not served a notice of intent to file litigation against appellees. After hearing argument on May 9, 1989, the trial court entered final summary judgment in favor of appellees. In essence, the court held that § 768.57 applied and that appellant had failed to comply with the statute's pre-filing notice requirements.

The revision has two advantages. Its second sentence throws less emphasis on the court's hearing, which has been relegated to a phrase, and focuses instead on the summary judgment itself. The reasons for the court's holding then get a sentence to themselves, as they deserve.

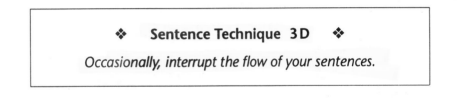

❖ **Sentence Technique 3 D** ❖

Occasionally, interrupt the flow of your sentences.

On page 5–8 we cautioned against unnecessarily frustrating a reader's desire to see subject, verb, and object or complement in one look, without having to hunt for them through the sentence. But the skillful insertion of a few words between these grammatical elements—or between any other words that normally abut—can help to underline a point. By forcing the reader to wait for something he is expecting, you give extra emphasis both to the intervening words and, when they finally come, to the words for which he has been waiting. We have already seen this example from Winston Churchill:

> On this day, the Luftwaffe, after two heavy attacks on the 14th, made its greatest concentrated effort in a resumed daylight attack on London.

You can achieve a similar effect by any kind of interruption to the sentence's flow, especially if the interruption is emphasized by punctuation. In the next sentence, from the same Churchillian passage, note how we are made to wait before we get the information that the word "and" promises:

It was one of the decisive battles of the war, and, like the Battle of Waterloo, it was on a Sunday.

This technique has a converse: Except for the sake of emphasis, do not interrupt a sentence's flow:

Original:

However, if, through fluctuations in exchange rates or upon some action by Worldco, the dollar equivalents of the obligations were to rise above $10,000,000, then Bigbank would, under the Agreement, be entitled to demand additional collateral.

Revision:

However, if the dollar equivalents of the obligations were to rise above $10,000,000, either through fluctuations in the exchange rates or upon some action by Worldco, then Bigbank would be entitled under the Agreement to demand additional collateral.

❖ **SENTENCE PRINCIPLE 4** ❖

Long sentences should be organized so that they do not exhaust the reader's attention span.

In the past few decades, many of the most popular how-to-write manuals told us that short sentences are always easier to read than long ones. This is true, but it is not the whole truth. Sophisticated readers do not have more trouble with a moderately long sentence, if it is well-constructed, than with a short one. In fact, knowing how to construct longer sentences properly is important, because sometimes they alone do justice to the precise relationships among a closely related group of facts or ideas. You can overdo it, of course. In general, avoid sentences that run more than four or five lines of type, and avoid more than two or three longer sentences in a row. But the ideal is not a string of short sentences unless you are creating a special effect, such as hammering home some crucial facts. Usually, the ideal is a mixture of short and moderately long in which the longer sentences are not much harder to read than the short. The exact mix will depend upon your audience and, to some degree, your own taste.

Long sentences are not easy to write, however. Not only do they have to be clear; they also have to avoid burying their key points. These problems are causes for concern but not pessimism, because there are techniques for writing a longer sentence effectively.

❖   **Sentence Technique 4A**   ❖

Break a long sentence into parts.

As a general proposition, a longer sentence is easier to read when it is built as a series of relatively brief parts, each a self-contained unit of meaning and each clearly marked off by punctuation. In such a sentence, the reader is never asked to swallow too many words in one bite. This is important because short-term memory cannot easily hold many words at a time, and it should not have to struggle to encompass all of a phrase or clause before transferring its meaning into long-term memory.

Original:

This case involves the novel issue of whether or not a minor is responsible for damages sustained by a restaurant in lost profits resulting from a liquor license suspension caused when the minor orally misrepresented her age to the owner of the restaurant who thereafter sold liquor to her.

Revision:

The issue in this case is novel: If a minor orally misrepresents her age to a restaurant owner who sells liquor to her, and as a result the owner has his liquor license suspended, is the minor responsible for the damages sustained by the restaurant in lost profits?

Sometimes you can improve a sentence simply by inserting punctuation:

Original:

Problems of perfection arise with leases of equipment not listed on the filing schedules usually because equipment was substituted after the original filing without an amended filing.

Revision:

Problems of perfection arise with leases of equipment not listed on the filing schedules, usually because equipment was substituted after the original filing without an amended filing.

More often, though, you will need to reconstruct the sentence by breaking one clause into two:

Original:

The potential appreciation is defined at the time the Contingent Payment Rights are issued in such a way as to allow the Holders to assess the value of the potential appreciation prior to entering into the Merger Agreement.

Revision:

When the Contingent Payment Rights are issued, "potential appreciation" is defined in a way that allows the Holders to assess its value before they enter into the Merger Agreement.

or

Because of the definition given to "potential appreciation" at the time the Contingent Payment Rights are issued, the Holders can assess its value before they enter into the Merger Agreement.

As in this case, you can often reconstruct the sentence simply by organizing it into a cause-and-effect relationship or a conditional one ("if . . . then"). Here is an example of the latter:

Original:

A creditor who holds a security interest in property transferable chiefly by lease because there is little or no market for sale of such property should receive as much protection as a creditor with an interest in property that can be sold.

Revision:

If a creditor holds a security interest in property transferable chiefly by lease because there is little or no market for a sale, the creditor should receive as much protection as a creditor with an interest in property that can be sold.

or

If a creditor holds a security interest in property that has little or no market for a sale, and is therefore transferable chiefly by lease, the creditor should receive . . . .

❖ **Sentence Technique 4B** ❖

Use repetition to remind the reader of the sentence's topic.

The following sentences use three different kinds of repetition. The first literally repeats a word; the second uses words that sum up, or offer a synonym for, what precedes them; the third uses pronouns to refer back to an earlier noun. In each case, the repetition is italicized:

(1) For several years the Supreme Court invented and developed legal theories that were excellent examples of the dangers of judicial activism, *theories* such as . . . .

(2) In the last five years population growth has dropped almost to zero, *a demographic event* that in years to come will have profound social implications.

(3) Although Justice X was well-known for his liberal political ideas, he always had the hint of a conservative style about him, *his* suits bearing the discreet marks of custom tailoring, *his* attitude toward women always courtly but distant.

❖ **Sentence Technique 4C** ❖

If some information in a long sentence is context for the rest, put the context first.

Many writers consistently put the context last for the same reasons that they consistently put last the "old info" that creates a link to the preceding sentence: Their minds are focused on the new nugget they want to deliver, and until they get it down on paper they have no time to think about its surroundings. A good writer, in contrast, trains himself to worry about the context first, here as at the other levels of organization. If he does not, he knows he will create annoying surprises for the reader. In the following example, note how you must reassess the sentence's early information in the light of a context announced only at its end:

Original:

A creditor is required under California's one-action rule to foreclose upon collateral before proceeding against the debtor's unsecured assets when a debtor's obligation is secured by real property.

Revision:

When a debtor's obligation is secured by real property, California's one-action rule requires the creditor to foreclose upon collateral before proceeding against the debtor's unsecured assets.

or:

Revision:

Under California's one-action rule, when a debtor's obligation is secured by real property, the creditor must foreclose upon collateral before proceeding against the debtor's unsecured assets.

The choice between the revisions depends upon the answer to one of the following questions (or, perhaps, both): Which revision offers the smoothest transition from the preceding sentence? Is the more informative context for the sentence the kind of debt or the California rule?

This technique also applies to a sequence of related statements—for example, when you want to contrast two perspectives or pieces of information:

Original:

The two cases plaintiff cites contain strong language in support of its position. Both cases are factually distinguishable from the present one, however.

This form hides the fact of contrast until very late. Moving the "however" from the end of the second sentence to its beginning would help. But in some contexts it would help even more to combine the two sentences into one, announcing the contrast at the very beginning:

Revision:

Although the two cases plaintiff cites do indeed contain strong language in support of its position, both cases are factually distinguishable from the present one.

As you may have noticed, when you put the context first you create other welcome changes:

Original:

May a nonparty collaterally attack the jurisdiction of a bankruptcy court that has rendered a decision under Bankruptcy Rule 7001 where the parties have proceeded by motion rather than an adversary proceeding?

Revision:

When parties in a bankruptcy have proceeded by motion rather than an adversary proceeding, and the bankruptcy court has rendered a decision under Bankruptcy Rule 7001, may a nonparty collaterally attack the court's jurisdiction?

As the contextual information moves to the front of the sentence, the most important information moves to the end, where it belongs. And the sentence falls into distinct parts, separated by punctuation. Good habits, it is pleasant to see, reinforce each other.

At the Chapter's beginning, we said we would end by pointing out situations in which even good writers often violate some basic rules of composing sentences. Here are our warnings:

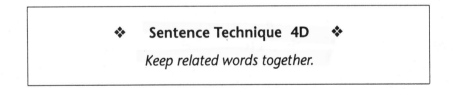

❖   **Sentence Technique 4D**   ❖

Keep related words together.

The longer and more complicated the sentence, the more likely that some modifying phrase will wander away from its proper mooring next to what it should modify. With good writers, the results are seldom fatal to the sentence's meaning, but they make it harder to read.

Original:

Confirmation discharges only the debtor's liability, not that of a nondebtor which may be liable as a joint tortfeasor or otherwise to creditors.

Revision:

Confirmation discharges only the debtor's liability, not that of a nondebtor which may be liable to creditors as a joint tortfeasor or otherwise.

or

Confirmation discharges only the debtor's liability to creditors, not that of a nondebtor which may be liable as a joint tortfeasor or otherwise.

Here is an amusing—and authentic—example of a badly organized sentence. It is the last sentence in a letter sent to a lawyer who shared it with us, recognizing how well it illustrated our point:

I apologize for the delay in getting this letter to you, but we had three out of four secretaries come down with some form of the flu all this week and two partners.

We suggest you revise this one yourself.

The word "only," incidentally, often floats loose from its proper place:

Original:

To prove yourself, you *only* have to jump through the first two hoops . . .

So far, this sentence means that the victim has to jump through the hoops as an alternative to doing something else (say, signing a pledge to bill 2000 hours a year). But the rest of the sentence says: ". . . not all six." What the writer means, then, should have been expressed as:

Revision:

To prove yourself, you have to jump through *only* the first two hoops, not all six.

Another common form of misplacement is what you may recall from long-ago classrooms as a dangling modifier. A standard classroom example is:

Original:

Sitting in the bathtub, the telephone rang.

The image is a cartoonist's delight, but it is not what the writer meant. An introductory phrase at the start of a sentence, especially if the phrase contains some form of a verb, attaches itself grammatically to the first noun in the rest of the sentence. Make sure that the first noun is in fact the one to which it should be attached. If it is not, there are easy cures:

Revision:

Sitting in the bathtub, I heard the phone ring.

or

While I was sitting in the bathtub, the telephone rang.

Here is an actual example of this problem:

Original:

Although incomplete in some respects, we wanted to distribute this draft for review.

Revision:

Although this draft is incomplete in some respects, we wanted to distribute it for review.

❖   **Sentence Technique 4E**   ❖

Express parallel ideas in parallel form.

Writers most often violate this rule in two ways.

(1) When joining two or more groups of words that constitute a list of items, they fail to put all groups into the same kind of grammatical container. The first may be an independent clause; the second a dependent clause; and so forth.

Original:

Courts have cited the following factors: (1) the assignment was contained in the granting clause of the mortgage; (2) the deed of trust was not explicit in stating that the creditor need not take possession or make demand before becoming entitled to the rents; and [here comes the problem] (3) the use of the words "as additional security," "for the purpose of securing," or their equivalents.

For the sake of parallelism, the third item should also be inside an independent clause, not a phrase:

Revision:

. . . and (3) the mortgage or deed of trust contained the words "as additional security," "for the purpose of securing," or their equivalents.

In addition to keeping the grammatical forms parallel, try to keep the wording as similar as possible:

Original:

The primary questions are: (1) whether the individual is a New York domiciliary, (2) if he has a permanent place of abode in New York, and (3) the number of days he is physically present in New York.

Revision:

The primary questions are: (1) whether the individual is a New York domiciliary, (2) whether he has a permanent place of abode in New York, and (3) whether he is physically present in New York for more than 180 days.

Here is a less obvious example of the problem:

Original:

The issue of good faith is most frequently raised in connection with the limited partnership debtor formed to invest in real property and which holds only one substantial asset.

Revision:

The issue of good faith is most frequently raised in connection with the limited partnership debtor which was formed to invest in real property and which holds only one substantial asset.

The second "which" could be omitted, still leaving the parallel structure of two verbs ("was formed" and "holds") following the first "which."

(2) Faulty parallels also arise because a word such as "either" or "both" is misplaced.

Original:

Rule 11f-6(c) is generally a basis for arguments *either* asserting that the proposal would require the registrant to violate its existing obligations or that the proposal's objective is too broad.

Revision:

Rule 11f-6(c) is generally a basis for arguments asserting *either* that the proposal would require the registrant to violate its existing obligations or that the proposal's objective is too broad.

❖ **Sentence Technique 4F** ❖

When a sentence contains a series of items, be careful about where you put the "and's" and "or's."

Danger lurks not when you have a series of single items (a, b, and c, for example), but when one of the items is itself a multi-part series (a, b-1 and b-2, and c, for example). The danger is significant because it arises from conceptual sloppiness, not just stylistic clumsiness. For an example, examine the sentence below. It is written as if it contains an "a, b, or c" series:

Original:

Megacorp objects to the Request because it is [a] overbroad, [b] unduly burdensome, and [c] asks for material which is neither relevant to the subject matter of this litigation nor reasonably calculated to lead to the discovery of admissible evidence.

It is written, in other words, as if three items follow the verb "is." In fact, only two follow "is"; the third follows another verb, "asks." To fix the syntax, then, the sentence should be revised to read:

Revision 1:

Megacorp objects to the Request because it [a] is overbroad and unduly burdensome and [b] asks for material which is neither relevant to the subject matter of this litigation nor reasonably calculated to lead to the discovery of admissible evidence.

But this revision does not go far enough: While it solves the syntactical problem, it fails to cure the underlying conceptual fuzziness. (The fuzziness arises, we suspect, from the rote repetition of a formulaic objection.) Conceptually, into how many categories do Megacorp's objections fall? The answer depends on the specifics of the document request and Megacorp's tactics for opposing it, but let's assume there are two categories. The sentence should then read as follows:

Revision 2:

Megacorp objects to the Request [a] because it is overbroad and therefore unduly burdensome, and [b] because it asks for material which is neither relevant to the subject matter of this litigation nor reasonably calculated to lead to the discovery of admissible evidence.

The addition of "therefore" binds together the parts of the first category; the repetition of "because it" more clearly separates the first category from the second.

We have lingered over this problem for two reasons. First, even good writers often have trouble spotting it. Second, it can sometimes lead to drastic consequences for a document's organization. If the writer of the sentence's original version went on to organize a memorandum of law to support the sentence's claim, how would he organize the memorandum? The chances are he would repeat the same conceptual error that afflicts the sentence, simply because its structure had imprinted itself in his thinking.

Here is a more complicated example of the same problem:

Original:

Generally, the capital and surplus restrictions require that at least 60 percent of the minimum capital or surplus investments be made in obligations of the United States, any state, any of New York State's counties, districts or municipalities, or certain mortgage loans on property in New York.

This sentence is written as if it lists four kinds of obligations: obligations of (1) the United States, (2) any state, (3) any of New York State's counties, districts or municipalities, or (4) certain mortgage loans on property in New York. In fact, the mortgage loans are not another type of governmental obligation, but a different category of investment. The sentence omitted a necessary "or," which is italicized in the revision:

Revision:

Generally, the capital and surplus restrictions require that at least 60 percent of the minimum capital or surplus investments be made either in obligations of the United States, any state, *or* any of New York State's counties, districts or municipalities, or in certain mortgage loans on property in New York.

This change makes the sentence say what the writer means, but the reader could use more help. Here is a clearer version:

Revision 2:

Generally, the capital and surplus restrictions require that at least 60 percent of the minimum capital or surplus investments be made in two types of investment: (1) obligations of the United States, any state, or any of New York State's counties, districts or municipalities, or (2) certain mortgage loans on property in New York.

One warning about making these kinds of revisions: Occasionally, you will have to rely on statutory or judicial language that suffers from the problem we have described. In these cases, you may have to mimic the language of your authority, as misshapen as it is. You should still make sure, however, that you do not allow its sloppiness to damage the clarity of your own thinking and organization.

Finally, remember that this discussion of sentence length did not begin by advocating long sentences over short ones. The best cure for a clumsy long sentence may be to chop it in half. This is an old truth, but lawyers still have trouble believing it. Here is yet another example:

Original:

The Tax Court held that the Regulation's provision that disclaimers be made within a "reasonable time" after the taxpayer first acquires "knowledge of the existence of the transfer" required Petitioners to have disclaimed their contingent remainder interests in 1957 (after the service of citations) rather than upon the death of the income beneficiary in 1974.

Revision:

The Regulation provides that disclaimers be made within a "reasonable time" after the taxpayer first acquires "knowledge of the existence of the transfer." As a result, the Tax Court held that the Petitioners were required to have disclaimed their contingent remainder interests in 1957, after the service of citations, rather than upon the death of the income beneficiary in 1974.

The structure of longer, more complicated sentences can be given several different labels, which we describe briefly in Appendix B, "A Brief Review of Syntax."

CHAPTER **6**

Bringing the Advice Together

WE HAVE NOW COVERED enough ground to warrant a pause to gain perspective on what lies behind. This Chapter will draw together some of the principles and techniques we have discussed to show how, in practice, they can be used to edit legal writing. To this end, we will perform and explain detailed edits of three short passages. Where our changes reflect judgment calls—as many of them do—you may disagree with us. Our explanations, however, along with your assessment of them, should illustrate what it means to think like a writer.

As we hope to show, it first means *seeing* like a writer. Those of you old enough to have grown up watching Westerns may recall a stock scene: As the cavalry patrol chases the bad guys, the Indian scout peers down at a patch of dust and says, "Three horses and a mule passed here two days ago, and the mule was carrying a big man with a bad leg." The scout had no better eyesight than the cavalrymen, but his profession had trained him to see what others missed. As a lawyer, you are trained to see legal problems—to "spot issues"—that are invisible to others, and then to use your understanding of the law to propose good, not just adequate, solutions. Similarly, as a writer and editor, you must learn to spot the places where you face an organizational or stylistic choice, and you must understand the principles that guide you to making a good choice among several acceptable alternatives.

Now, we return to the chase of the bad guys.

EXAMPLE 1

Original:

The reason that funded programs have been less utilized than un-funded programs is that under the tax law if an employee is given a nonforfeitable interest in a nonqualified trust she will experience immediate taxation on the amounts set aside for her.

Problems:

- Long sentence with no interior punctuation
- Weak subject and verb ("reason . . . is")
- Sentence begins with "The reason that" formula

Any one of these symptoms alone should lead you to fix the sentence.

Revision:

③+④
because of
their tax
disadvantages.

①   F   used ② often,

~~The reason that~~ funded programs have been less ~~utilized~~ than un-funded programs ~~is that under the tax law~~ If an employee is given a nonforfeitable interest in a nonqualified trust she will ~~experience immediate taxation~~ on the amounts set aside for her.

⑤
immediately
be taxed

The techniques:

1. Get rid of "The reason that," which is throat-clearing.
2. "Less utilized" is pretentious; change to more familiar "used less often."
3. Break the sentence into two.
4. Use "tax disadvantages" to set the context, identifying the kind of point you are making before providing the details.
5. Change "experience immediate taxation," because it sounds unidiomatic.

Second thoughts:

③ — ①   ② ones

Funded programs *have been used* less often than unfunded ~~programs~~ because of *their* tax disadvantages. If an employee is given a nonforfeitable interest in a nonqualified trust he will *be taxed immediately* on the amounts set aside for him.

④ :

⑤ ⑦ ⑥

The judgment calls:

1. Change the passive to active? No, the emphasis here should remain on the programs, not their users.
2. Replace "programs" with a pronoun, to avoid repetition? Yes, but another close call. Lawyers are trained to avoid pronouns because they create ambiguity if used sloppily. If the audience is legal and conservative, keep the repetition.
3. Is there a chance that "their" might be momentarily taken to refer to the preceding noun ("unfunded programs")? No.
4. Replace the period with a colon? Perhaps. The colon signals that the next sentence will name the disadvantage. But it is a close call. The modern tendency is to use fewer colons and semicolons.
5. Insert a comma between the sentence's two clauses.
6. Move the adverb "immediately" to the end of the verb rather than the middle.

Original continued:

Funded programs have been used less often than unfunded ones because of their tax disadvantages. If an employee is given a nonforfeitable interest in a nonqualified trust, he will be taxed immediately on the amounts set aside for him. **Furthermore, the complex and onerous requirements of Title I of ERISA would normally apply to a funded program.**

Trouble:

- We discover too late that funded programs have two kinds of disadvantages.
- The words that link the third sentence to the second appear at its end, not at its beginning.

Revision:

Funded programs have been used less often than unfunded ones for two reasons. First, they have tax disadvantages: If an employee is given a nonforfeitable interest in a nonqualified trust, he will be taxed immediately on the amounts set aside for him. Second, they are normally subject to the complex and onerous requirements of Title I of ERISA.

Judgment calls:

1. Is the "first"/"second" language too heavy-handed? A matter of taste. You could omit "first" and, instead of "second," use "furthermore."

2. At the beginning of the last sentence, does "they" have a clear referent? It refers to funded programs, but the closest preceding plural noun is "amounts." Is this a problem? No. Especially because the structure of the sentence parallels the structure of the second sentence, no one will have even a momentary doubt about what "they" refers to.

EXAMPLE 2

Original:

You have asked me to discuss the extent to which a settlor of a personal trust created under Delaware law may retain certain powers in various combinations without causing the assets of the trust to be subject to the rights of the settlor's creditors. While various combinations of retained powers have been considered, it does not appear that the various combinations produce results different from any single power. There is very little Delaware law which deals with this subject, and where there is no Delaware authority, I have turned to cases from other jurisdictions and to authorities such as the Restatement, Scott and Bogert that are generally accepted in Delaware.

To begin with, it should be pointed out that spendthrift trusts in Delaware are the subject of statute. That statute, 12 *Del.C.* § 3536, provides as follows:

> (a) The creditors of a beneficiary of a trust shall have only such rights against such beneficiary's interest in the trust . . . .

Problems with the first paragraph:

- The ambitious, but legitimate, purpose of this paragraph is to introduce and summarize the question, answer, and analysis of a memorandum. But it fails because each sentence is long and difficult.
- The sentences switch back and forth between active and passive voice.

Revision of first sentence (allowing it to continue its function of stating the question):

First attempt:

You have asked me to discuss an issue of Delaware trust law involving a settlor of a personal trust who retains certain powers over the trust property: How much and what kinds of power may the settlor retain while still insulating the property from the claims of his or her creditors?

Problems:

- While this revision makes the statement of the question itself more explicit, and shorter and easier to comprehend, it creates a long introduction that may dissipate the reader's attention. This depends on the audience. A Delaware trust and estates lawyer will not have a serious problem with the sentence. But the memorandum was written by an associate in a Delaware firm for lawyers in other states, many of whom practice principally in areas other than trusts.

Second attempt:

You have asked me to discuss an issue of Delaware trust law: How much power, and what kinds of power, over trust property may the settlor of a personal trust retain, while still insulating that property from the claims of his or her creditors?

Discussion:

– The introduction leading to the question is now very short and direct, and thus better suited to an audience for whom Delaware trust law is alien territory.
– Although the question itself is longer, the sentence is broken into manageable sections, separated by punctuation and knitted together with repeated key words (*e.g.,* "power" and "property").
– Should "How much power, and what kinds of power, over trust property" be changed to "How much power over trust property, and what kinds of power"? Another judgment call. The latter is a little more idiomatic, and reads more smoothly. But the former is a kind of syntax to which lawyers are accustomed.
– Should the phrase "insulate that property" be shortened to "insulate it"? A judgment call. Leaving in the phrase "that property" probably allows readers to wade through the question a bit more easily, since they do not have to worry about pronoun references.
– Is the phrase "his or her" necessary? Probably. If it is eliminated, the reference of "claims of creditors" becomes more general than the writer intends—encompassing, for example, the trust's creditors.

Revision of second sentence (again allowing it to serve as the summary answer to the question):

I have considered a range of retained powers, and various combinations of them, and have found that the result is consistent: . . . .

Discussion:

The second sentence now has a structure parallel to the first:

- It begins in the first person, and is in active rather than passive voice.
- It is broken up into more readable segments.
- It uses a colon to announce the answer itself, which we can now see is missing. That summary answer should be part of the memo's introduction.

Revision of third sentence (the summary of the memorandum's analysis):

However, Delaware has very little law on this subject. Where it lacks direct authority, I have turned to cases from other jurisdictions and to scholarly authorities generally accepted in Delaware, such as the Restatement and the treatises by Scott and Bogert.

Discussion:

- The original version's one sentence is now two.
- The first of these is short, and contrasts with longer ones before and after it; this emphasizes its content.
- The first sentence begins with "however" to announce immediately its change in perspective.
- The first sentence's verb is in active voice rather than "throat clearing" form.
- The second sentence begins with "Where it . . ." to link it quickly and directly to the preceding one.
- The opening of the second sentence is also in the active voice.
- The end of the second sentence is restructured to remove the "such as . . ." phrase from the middle of the description of "authorities generally accepted. . . ."

Here is the entire revised paragraph:

You have asked me to discuss an issue of Delaware trust law: How much power, and what kinds of power, over trust property may the settlor of a personal trust retain, while still insulating that property from the claims of his or her creditors? I have considered a range of retained powers, and various combinations of them, and have found that the result is consistent: . . . . However, Delaware has very little law on this subject. Where it lacks direct authority, I have turned to cases from other jurisdictions and to scholarly authorities generally accepted in Delaware, such as the Restatement and the treatises by Scott and Bogert.

The second paragraph also has problems, which we will point out without attempting a revision. Here is its beginning again:

> To begin with, it should be pointed out that spendthrift trusts in Delaware are the subject of statute. That statute, 12 *Del.C.* § 3536, provides as follows:
>
> > (a) The creditors of a beneficiary of a trust shall have only such rights against such beneficiary's interest in the trust . . . .

Problems:

- The first nine words are unnecessary.
- The paragraph opens by referring to "spendthrift trusts," which is new information. The link between this paragraph and the first is a mystery, unless the reader happens to know as much about trust law as the writer. Even then the link is at best very weak.
- The statute quoted continues for many more lines. Thus, its introduction—"provides as follows"—is inadequate. Instead, the introduction should summarize the statute's key points. This serves either of two functions: It allows the reader to skip the statutory language if she is in a hurry; or, if she does read the statute, the more comprehensive introduction reinforces its substance because she looks for the key points announced in advance.

EXAMPLE 3

Original:

Re: *Amendment of Rule 10b-6*

Dear Jane:

On January 14, 1987, the Securities and Exchange Commission (the "Commission") adopted a number of amendments to Rule 10b-6 (the "Rule") of the Securities Exchange Act of 1934 (the "Exchange Act"), which amendments will become effective as of March 1, 1987. As you know, the Rule is an antimanipulative rule that prohibits, subject to certain exceptions, persons engaged in a distribution of securities from bidding for or purchasing, or inducing others to bid for or purchase, such securities or any related securities until they have completed their participation in the distribution. The purpose of the Rule is to prevent participants in a distribution from artificially conditioning the market for the securities in order to facilitate the distribution of such securities.

The Rule does contain, however, a list of narrowly defined exceptions for transactions that are intended to permit an orderly distribution of securities or limit disruption in the market for the securities being distributed. The amendments adopted to the Rule on January 14 contain a number of important expansions of these exceptions, the most important of which concern cooling-off periods for such solicited brokerage transactions and exercises of call options.

Problems:

– The first sentence begins and ends with specific dates, thereby emphasizing them, but we do not know why it does so. On the face of the document, the dates do not seem very important.
– The letter never states its "point" explicitly. Why should Jane spend time reading this document?
– The parentheticals in the opening sentence are distracting. They are also unhelpful: No other "Commission" or "Exchange Act" is ever discussed, making these parentheticals unnecessary, while other rules *are* discussed, making later references to "the Rule" confusing.
– In the first paragraph, the information in the second and third sentences violates Organizational Principle I, Form A, by putting detail before context. The two sentences move from the "specific" to the "general"—from particular prohibitions to the reasons for those prohibitions—which is usually the wrong order in which to present information in an expository document.

- In the second paragraph, the information in the two sentences seems to be in the correct order, but the structure of the preceding paragraph makes the transition to this paragraph difficult.
- The tone of the letter is formal and distant, in contrast to the first name familiarity of the opening ("Dear Jane" rather than "Dear Ms. Smith"). The letter does, however, appear to be addressed to someone well-acquainted with securities law ("As you know . . ."), and it therefore is probably serving the purpose of a formal notification of changes in those laws. But the reader need not be forced to consume prose that takes on the stilted and depersonalized character of the regulations it is describing.

These problems may require more than one edit. Here is a first attempt:

Revision 1:

Re: *Amendment of Rule 10b-6* ①

Dear Jane: ②

On January 14, 1987, the Securities and Exchange Commission (the "Commission") adopted a number of amendments to Rule 10b-6 (the "Rule") of the Securities Exchange Act of 1934 (the "Exchange Act"), which amendments will become effective as of March 1, 1987. As you know, The Rule is an antimanipulative rule that prohibits, subject to certain exceptions, persons engaged in a distribution of securities from bidding for or purchasing, or inducing others to bid for or purchase, such securities or any related securities until they have completed their participation in the distribution. The purpose of the Rule is to prevent participants in a distribution from artificially conditioning the market for the securities in order to facilitate the distribution of such securities.

The Rule does contain, however, a list of narrowly defined exceptions for transactions that are intended to permit an orderly distribution of securities or limit disruption in the market for the securities being distributed. The amendments adopted to the Rule on January 14 contain a number of important expansions of these exceptions, the most important of which concern cooling-off periods for such solicited brokerage transactions and exercises of call options.

Handwritten annotations:
- ③ The purpose of this letter is to apprise you of those amendments and their importance to corporate brokerage transactions.
- (therefore)
- of securities
- enhancing
- at
- The amendments expand
- concern the exceptions to the Rule, which
- for present purposes
- ④

Comments:

1. The dates in the first sentence have been noted for further discussion with the writer, but not changed at this point.

2. The parentheticals have been removed. If these efforts at precision do in fact prove necessary or useful to the letter, they can be inserted the second time the terms appear rather than the first, to keep the first sentence from becoming cluttered and clumsy.

3. A statement of the letter's purpose has been added.

4. This statement creates an introduction that can now be its own paragraph. The second paragraph can in turn become a longer one that unites the discussion of Rule 10b-6 and its recent amendments.

5. The changes to the wording of the sentences remove some unnecessary repetition but do not alter the letter's formal tone substantially.

Here is how the letter would now read:

Retyped Revision 1:

Re: *Amendment of Rule 10b-6*

Dear Jane:

On January 14, 1987, the Securities and Exchange Commission adopted a number of amendments to Rule 10b-6 of the Securities Exchange Act of 1934, which amendments will become effective on March 1, 1987. The purpose of this letter is to apprise you of those amendments and their importance to corporate brokerage transactions.

As you know, the purpose of the Rule is to prevent participants in a distribution of securities from artificially enhancing the market for that distribution. The Rule therefore prohibits, subject to certain exceptions, persons engaged in a distribution of securities from bidding for or purchasing, or inducing others to bid for or purchase, such securities or any related securities until they have completed their participation in the distribution. The amendments adopted on January 14 concern the exceptions to the Rule, which are intended to permit an orderly distribution of securities or to limit disruption in the market for the securities being distributed. The amendments expand these exceptions, the most important of which for present purposes concern cooling-off periods for solicited brokerage transactions and exercises of call options.

A second look, however, suggests that more can be done to improve the letter:

Comments on Revision 1:

– The tone is probably still too formal for its audience.

- The statement of the letter's purpose is not yet specific enough for a business client.
- With a more complete statement of purpose, the structure of the letter—beginning with background discussion of the nature and purpose of these securities laws, and then moving to their application to more specific kinds of transactions—might be presented more clearly.

This leads to another edit:

Revision 2:

Dear Jane:

The Securities and Exchange Commission recently adopted a number of amendments to Rule 10b-6 of the Securities Exchange Act of 1934. These amendments, which become effective as of March 1, expand the exceptions to the Rule's general prohibition against persons engaged in a distribution of securities entering the market for them. Because these changes will affect your firm's work, we are providing the following analysis of their impact.

Among the changes, these are the most important for your firm:

(1) . . .

(2) . . .

(3) . . .

Background. The changes do not alter the Rule's purpose of preventing persons engaged in a distribution from artificially enhancing the market for the securities to facilitate their distribution. In general, the Rule prohibits these persons from bidding for or purchasing the securities or related securities, or inducing others to bid for or purchase them. The prohibition extends for as long as a person continues to participate in the distribution.

Before the amendments, however, the Rule contained only some narrow exceptions to these prohibitions, for transactions intended to permit an orderly distribution of securities or to limit disruption in the market for them. The amendments have significantly expanded the exceptions.

Even this edit, however, may not capture the right tone for communicating with a client the writer knows well enough to refer to as "Jane." If the situation warrants, she could write something much more personal and direct:

Revision 3:

Dear Jane:

Good news! The Securities and Exchange Commission has finally adopted the changes to Rule 10b-6 that we discussed some time ago. We now have better answers to a number of troubling questions, such as . . .

CHAPTER 7

Using Words and Punctuation

IN THE PREVIOUS CHAPTER, we considered words as parts of sentences—subjects and verbs, phrases and clauses, points of natural emphasis, and so on. This Chapter focuses on words outside the context of any sentence. It also deals briefly with punctuation as an aid to clarity.

Words: Precision and Brevity

When you edit at the level of words, you are almost always concerned with one of two issues: either precision (saying exactly what you mean) or brevity (saying it efficiently). The first two sections below are about the former. The first discusses the embarrassment of riches presented by our language, while the next focuses on a particular embarrassment of legal writing: nominalization. The third section then switches to the struggle to be concise.

Precision and Diction

> The difference between the almost right word and the right word is like the difference between the lightning bug and lightning.
>
> —Mark Twain

Twain's remark is typically colorful, but, at the risk of sounding un-American, we disagree. The difference between two similar words is seldom that dramatic. It is more often like the difference between an alligator and a crocodile: For many (perhaps most) readers, the distinction is obscure or unimportant, but for some the failure to observe it makes the writer sound a bit foolish. Those who write primarily for professional, well-educated audiences must assume that their readers are in the latter category, and must therefore choose their words with particular care. This sort of attention to detail is not mere window dressing or snobbishness; it is an important sign of one's professional attitude. Thus:

❖ WORD PRINCIPLE 1 ❖

*Because English vocabulary is so rich, good
writers must choose their words carefully.*

In English, choosing the right word can be particularly challenging. Our language contains many pairs or groups of words that have the same, or very similar, meanings. You can "buy" a "car" or "purchase" an "automobile," "talk" to your "lawyer" or "converse" with your "attorney," "initiate" a project or "begin" it. This overlapping gives us two advantages. First, we can indicate formality or informality by choosing the longer or shorter of two synonyms. If we write about "purchasing an automobile," for example, we dress the occasion in fancier clothes than if we write about "buying a car." Second, we can indicate subtle and precise shades of meaning because words often accepted as synonyms usually have different connotations.

For example, the dictionary offers several words that mean "to communicate orally": "speak," "talk," "discuss," "converse," and "consult," among others. But a careful writer will not treat them as interchangeable. Each implies a distinct kind of communication. If a client says she spoke to her lawyer about a problem, she suggests that the communication was largely one-sided, a matter of informing the lawyer rather than getting advice from her. If the client says that she and her lawyer talked, then she implies that an exchange occurred, but that it remained fairly casual. If the two of them discussed the problem, the exchange was more complex, more formal, and perhaps more important. If the client consulted her lawyer, then she was searching for serious professional advice. None of these connotations is stable through time or universally recognized at any one time. But they exist, even if people disagree about the precise connotations some words carry. Writers thus have a duty to use the word that conveys a meaning precisely, rather than the first word that comes to mind as a rough approximation.

Why is our vocabulary so rich? Largely because it has added so many words from different languages to the Anglo-Saxon vocabulary with which it began. We owe large debts, for example, to both the Scandinavians who settled parts of England in the ninth century and the French-speaking Normans who conquered England in the eleventh century. As a result, we have at our disposal hundreds of near-synonyms such as "raise" (Norse) and "rear" (Anglo-Saxon); "want" (Norse), "wish" (Anglo-Saxon), and "desire" (French); "possess" and "own"; "reveal" and "show"; and, to return to an earlier example, "purchase" and "buy." (In each of the last pairs, the shorter word derives from Anglo-Saxon, the longer from Old French.)

If English had little choice but to add a Scandinavian and Norman vocabulary to its Anglo-Saxon core, it has also been open-minded about borrowing words from other languages. During the centuries when Latin was the most prestigious language and the international language of the educated classes, English lifted from it such words as "punctual," "occult," and "lapidary," among many others. In later centuries, dozens of European, Asian and African languages have contributed to our vocabulary. As a result, although almost all of the 200 words we use most frequently are Anglo-Saxon in origin, only about a third of our total vocabulary is.

One result of our melting-pot vocabulary, incidentally, is that old-fashioned legal language is replete with such pairs and triplets as "will and testament," "goods and chattels," and "give, devise, and bequeath." This type of repetition arose partly because of the need to make matters clear in more than one language. (As David Mellinkoff[*] points out, it also arose partly from a medieval fashion of doubling words even from the same language. "Have" and "hold," for example, both come from Anglo-Saxon roots.)

In the hands of a careful writer, the richness of our vocabulary makes possible a precision and flexibility of meaning few other languages can achieve. But it also allows a careless writer to fill her prose with multi-syllabic, pretentious words, and to blur her meaning by settling for a near-synonym rather than an exact word. To guard against these dangers, you should develop the following three habits.

---

[*] D. Melinkoff, *The Language of the Law* 121–22 (1963).

❖   **Word Technique 1A**   ❖

Choose an appropriate level of formality.

Avoid being seduced into pretentiousness by the legal prose you read. This is not easy, and we therefore give it more specific attention in Chapter 8, in the context of the character of your writing.

Some people, of course, have the opposite problem: They fail to adapt to a professional context—as the following story demonstrates.

> After a young lawyer had completed a lengthy oral argument, the judge asked him to visit the judge's chambers later in the day.
>
> "Young man," the judge began at their meeting, "you presented a fine argument today—well-reasoned and persuasive."
>
> As the young lawyer was about to relax and say "thank you, your Honor," the judge continued: "But I must point out to you that you used a couple of words throughout your presentation that I believe are inappropriate and distracting. And those words are 'awesome' and 'gross.' "
>
> The young lawyer, who had been listening intently, showed no reaction when the judge had finished speaking. Finally, after several seconds of silence, he shifted in his seat and, hesitantly, said, "Uh, thank you, your Honor, for bringing this to my attention. Now, what are those two words you want me to avoid?"

You may have to think about this for a minute.

❖   **Word Technique 1B**   ❖

When you have a choice between two or more words, consider the nuances that separate them.

Curiously, even though every lawyer knows that good legal analysis requires mental precision, many are precise in their choice of words only when the words refer to legal concepts. Outside that vocabulary, they relax and become sloppy. Here is a short list of common errors of imprecise terminology.

❖   Writing *feel* when you mean *think* or *believe*.

❖ Writing *verbal* when you mean *oral.*

❖ Writing *alibi* when you mean *excuse.*

❖ Writing *like* when you mean *as. Like* introduces noun phrases; *as* connects clauses (for example, "look like a fox" vs. "think as cunning foxes think").

❖ Writing *infer* when you mean *imply* (*imply* is to make a suggestion; *infer* is to receive it).

❖ Writing *comprise* when you mean *compose* (*comprise* means *encompass*; *compose* means *form*).

❖ Writing *assume* when you mean *presume.*

❖ Writing *disinterested* if you mean *uninterested* (a judge should be disinterested, but not uninterested, in the case before her).

❖ Confusing *finding* and *holding.* A *finding* is the determination of an issue of fact. The word should not be used to refer to a court's *holding* on a matter of law.

❖ Writing *ruling* when you mean *holding* (a judge *rules* on motions and objections to evidence; ultimately she *holds* for the plaintiff or for the defendant).

❖ Writing *alternate* when you mean *alternative*, or vice versa. *Alternate* refers to things that follow in succession ("They serve in alternate years."). *Alternative* refers to mutually exclusive choices ("You must choose one of the alternatives by tomorrow."). Some purists insist that "alternative" should only be used when there are no more than two choices, but they are in a minority.

❖ Writing *continuous* when you mean *continual. Continuous* should refer to an uninterrupted extent of time or space; continual should refer to an intermittently repeated activity ("He was continually opening and closing the window.").

The *American Heritage Dictionary* and *Webster's International Dictionary* do an expert job of defining the shades of meaning that separate near-synonyms, and we suggest you turn to one of them whenever you are in doubt.

> ❖ **Word Technique 1C** ❖
>
> *When choosing between synonyms,*
> *ordinarily choose the simpler and shorter.*

The reasons are obvious enough to need no explanation.

Precision and Nominalization

When we choose words, English gives us one type of choice that often causes trouble. As you may recall from the earlier discussion of emphasizing action through active verbs, our language is full of words that can, with a change of spelling, work as either verbs or nouns. That means we can often replace a verb with a group of words based on a noun. This "nominalization" wastes words and robs prose of the vigor and clarity that strong, simple verbs impart. Hence, a second principle:

> ❖ **WORD PRINCIPLE 2** ❖
>
> *In general, actions should be expressed*
> *in verbs, not in nouns or adjectives.*

Here are examples:

EXAMPLE 1

Original:

The manager said he would *implement a rearrangement* of the workload *as an encouragement to* increased productivity.

Revision:

The manager said he would *rearrange* the workload *to encourage* increased productivity.

EXAMPLE 2

Original:

The *intention* of the parties was that the *resolution* of disputes should be governed by the application of New York law in a New York forum.

Revision:

The parties *intended* that disputes should be *resolved* by applying New York law in a New York forum.

Lawyers seem particularly prone to nominalization, but not simply because they are prone to stylistic pretentiousness. In legal writing the frequency of nominalization arises more fundamentally from the nature of legal reasoning. Lawyers have been trained to think in conceptual categories like "contract," "tort," and so on, categories that amalgamate instances of human interaction into identifiable sets. Lawyers therefore reason first in terms of noun-like summary entities that have been given specific legal labels ("crime," "trust," "loan"). They then try to divide and redivide these categories into subcategories as they approach the precise problem at hand. Consequently, lawyers, much to the amazement of laypersons, are far more apt to sense a distinction between the police "investigating" an incident and the police "conducting an investigation." The noun may refer to a range of legal detail—for example, certain required procedural steps—that the verb does not.

In some cases, then, nominalization is justified because the noun encapsulates a concept defined by a set of established elements.[*] In other cases, though, you should avoid this mode of writing because it has an inescapable

---

[*] This idea that words, legal or otherwise, are labels for sets of related examples is important to legal analysis, but it is beyond the scope of this book. The relevance of this linguistic theory to law can be summarized very briefly as follows: Significant legal concepts embodied in single terms (like property, liberty, equality, contract, securities, and so on) have an underlying linguistic structure that can be used to organize arguments involving any of them. All words are, of course, "ambiguous" to some degree, but their "open texture," as H.L.A. Hart called it, does not mean that words can mean anything and everything. Instead, ambiguity is not only limited, it has an order to it that can be exploited analytically. If you have some interest in seeing this approach in action, you could start with the following: Terrell, " 'Property', 'Due Process', and the Distinction Between Definition and Theory in Legal Analysis," 70 *Geo. L. J.* 861 (1982); Westen, "The Empty Idea of Equality," 95 *Harv. L. Rev.* 537 (1982); Westen, " 'Freedom' and 'Coercion'—Virtue Words and Vice Words," 1985 *Duke L. J.* 541; Terrell, "Conceptual Analysis and the Virtues and Vices of Professor Westen's Linguistics," 1986 *Duke L. J.* 660.

disadvantage: If you express important actions in nouns or adjectives rather than verbs, you make your sentences longer, less vigorous, and usually less clear.

Another form of this disease affects adverbs. For example, the New York State plain-English statute requires lawyers to write consumer contracts "in a clear and cogent manner." If the physician had been able to cure herself, she would have instead written "clearly and cogently."

Below is a more complete list of examples, some of which may have crept into your writing:

Shorten these:	*to these:*
have a tendency to	tend to
have a preference for	prefer
give permission to	allow, permit
give information to	inform
have need for	need
make application to	apply
make inquiry regarding	inquire
make note of	note
exhibits a tendency	tends
made the proposal	proposed
arrived at an estimate	estimated
gave approval	approved
make a decision	decide
it is obvious that	obviously (or omit altogether)
put the emphasis on	emphasize
give an indication of	indicate
have an understanding of	understand
make a comparison of	compare
is reflective of	reflects
accomplish (make) a change	change
take into consideration, take into account, give consideration to	consider
has the ability to, is in a position to	is able to, can
be in favor of	support
is desirous of	wants

be of the opinion that	think, believe
be of the same opinion, to be in agreement with, agree	
give assistance to	assist, help, aid
reach a conclusion	conclude
for the purpose of educating	to educate
take action	act
had occasion to be	was

Brevity

If clarity is partly a matter of choosing the right words, it is also a matter of using no more of them than necessary:

❖ **WORD PRINCIPLE 3** ❖

The fewer the words, the greater the impact (usually).

Brevity depends more on willpower than technique. When writing is noticeably verbose, the problem often arises from one or both of the following roots, neither of which can be attacked merely by technical means. First, the writer has not focused on the need for brevity when she edits. Initial drafts are always verbose. Subsequent drafts will be better only if you accept that inevitable fact and dedicate yourself to cutting words mercilessly. Second, many writers feel—and here we do mean "feel," for the impression seldom rises to the level of a thought—that longer is more impressive and more persuasive. In an analysis, they repeat a point in different forms. In a sentence, they add filler words and repeat information from earlier sentences. For some writers, as for some courtroom lawyers, the most difficult lesson to learn is when to shut up and sit down. To learn it well, paradoxically, we often have to gain confidence in the power of our words. If we believe that what we think and write has significance, and is correct, then we are more willing to put our faith in a single clear statement of each point. If we lack this confidence, we are tempted to pile words on top of words, trying to make up in quantity what we suspect our analysis lacks in quality.

The best cure for verbosity of this type is to read someone like Justice Holmes, whose style demonstrates that strength and dignity result from brevity. Beyond this advice, there is not much we can do to help: It is up to you.

Some forms of verbosity, however, do result from problems that are less fundamental and more technical. As we saw in Chapter 5, a badly constructed sentence is also likely to be a wordy one. Even in a well-constructed sentence, we often see excrescences that result from the writer's having fallen into the habit, in specific situations, of using several words when one or two would serve, and serve better. The techniques below focus on the types of verbose word clusters that most often appear in legal writing.

❖   **Word Technique 3A**   ❖

Avoid "stretched connections" (or compound prepositions).

The important words in a sentence often have to be glued together by prepositions, conjunctions, and adverbs. English sometimes offers a choice between a simple, one-word spot of glue and an obtrusive blob of several words. For example, you can write: "I consulted a lawyer *with regard to* the accident" or "I consulted a lawyer *about* the accident."

Here is a list (far from complete) of similar choices:

Simplify these:	*to these:*
at that point in time	then
at this point in time, in the present circumstances	now, at this point, at present
by means of	by
by reason of	because of
despite the fact that	although
due to the fact that, in as much as, in light of the fact that, on the grounds that	because, since
during the time that	while
for the price of $100	for $100
for the purpose of	to, for
for the reason that	because

inasmuch as	because
in connection with	about, with, for
in favor of	for
in order that x might	for x to
in relation to	about, concerning
in the course of, during the course of	during
in the event of, if it should happen	if
in the majority of instances	usually
in the near future	soon
made up out of	made of
on a regular basis	regularly
on the basis of	because of
on the order of	about
on the part of	by
pertaining to, in regard to, with reference to, with respect to, in relation to	about, of, on, for
prior to	before
situated in	in
starting out with	starting with
start up	start
subsequent to	after
supposing that	if
the fact that	that
the question of whether, whether or not, as to whether	whether
with a view to	to
with respect to, with regard to, with reference to	about, concerning
with the exception of	except for

As you may have noticed, "about" and "because" are the simple connectives lawyers most often avoid.

❖ **Word Technique 3B** ❖

Avoid strings of prepositional phrases.

Even one-word prepositions can clutter a sentence distractingly if they occur in a string of prepositional phrases. They can also force you into substituting nouns for verbs, as the examples below illustrate. Removing these strings will always produce a clearer as well as shorter sentence.

EXAMPLE 1

Original:

The amount *of* damages is determined *by* the measurement *of* the profit the dealer would have made *by* the sale *of* the car.

Revision:

The amount of damages is determined by measuring the profit the dealer would have made by selling the car.

or

The damages are determined by measuring the profit the dealer would have made had she sold the car.

or

The damages are the profit the dealer . . .

EXAMPLE 2

Original:

We have considered the appellant's argument that the trial court's denial of the admission of the report in question into evidence is reversible error.

Revision:

We have considered the appellant's argument that the trial court committed reversible error by refusing to admit this report into evidence.

7–12

❖ **Word Technique 3C** ❖

Avoid avoiding apostrophes.

A special form of connective bloat occurs because lawyers tend to avoid apostrophes. They will usually write, "The property belonging to the defendant . . . ." (or "The property of the defendant . . . ."), rather than "The defendant's property . . . ." The last version may once have been too informal for legal writing, but it certainly is not now.

❖ **Word Technique 3D** ❖

Avoid redundant phrasing, legal or otherwise.

Some redundancies are classically legal, as discussed earlier in this Chapter:

Do not *alter or change* . . . .

You must *cease and desist* . . . .

It is of the same *force and effect* . . . .

Others can arise in any kind of writing:

Shorten these:	*to these:*
absolutely essential	essential
close proximity to	close to
completely eliminated	eliminated
necessary requisite	necessary
general consensus	consensus
join together	join
prior experience	experience
refer back	refer
will in the future	will
basic essentials	essentials
advance planning	planning
visible to the eye	visible

tall skyscrapers	skyscrapers
circle around	circle
square in shape	square
worthy of merit	worthy

❖ **Word Technique 3E** ❖

Avoid unnecessary repetition.

Because lawyers want to avoid ambiguity, they are careful to identify a person, thing, or event at each reference. If this admirable caution becomes thoughtless habit, it lards legal writing with words that repeat information the reader already knows. This is irritating because it suggests either that the writer has a low opinion of the reader's intelligence or that the writer has not put much of her own intelligence into her work.

In the following example, the words in brackets are unnecessary:

Jones' alternative motion to transfer venue [of this case from this district] to the District of West Dakota is predicated on the interests of justice and the more convenient nature of that forum for the parties. A transfer [of the case to the District of West Dakota] is in the interests of justice because. . . .

If such repetitiousness becomes habitual, it can result in this kind of writing:

Original:

Furthermore, 10b-7 prohibits anyone from stabilizing a security at a price higher than the current independent bid price for such security. However, no court has yet determined whether the current independent bid price would be the price at the time of the writing of the option or at the time of the exercise of the option. A Rule 10b-7 defense would succeed only if the court interpreted the current independent bid price to be the price at the time of the writing of the option.

Revision:

Furthermore, 10b-7 prohibits anyone from stabilizing a security at a price higher than the current independent bid price. However, no court has yet determined whether this price would be the price at the time of the option's writing or at the time of its exercise. A Rule 10b-7 defense would succeed only if the court chose the first interpretation. [59 words instead of 84]

Like all the principles this book discusses, the principle of concision has to be applied with intelligent judgment. The shortest way is not always the best. Occasionally, you may want to lengthen a sentence a little to improve its rhythm, or to connect it more smoothly to the preceding one, or to clarify an over-condensed idea. As we stressed earlier, brevity is not simply a matter of counting words. It is not words you are trying to conserve (the supply, after all, is inexhaustible), but the reader's time and energy. For efficient writing, then, the right criterion is not how many words must be read, but how long it takes to understand them. Sometimes that process is accelerated by *adding* words, not subtracting them.

We warn you especially about one form of overcondensation that makes more work for the reader: stringing together two or more nouns to serve as a single adjective before a noun.

Original:

Defendant filed its pretrial document identification requests.

This sequence outrages the normal structure of English, and a reader will have to change it back into idiomatic English to absorb the information.* The reprocessing will occur subconsciously, unless the problem is especially bad, but it is still time-wasting and tiring. By adding some words, you make the prose more efficient:

---

* The King of Adjective Strings is not in fact some misguided lawyer, but a famous author: Dr. Seuss. If you are a parent, you already know that the problem we describe is, of course, the "tweetle beetle syndrome," a malady deriving its name from an inspired contortion of communication appearing in *Fox in Socks*. The incident begins innocently enough: "What do you know about tweetle beetles?" "Well, when tweetle beetles fight, it's called a tweetle beetle battle. And when they battle in a puddle, it's a tweetle beetle puddle battle." But with a few more layers of description, this becomes: "And when beetles fight these battles in a bottle with their paddles, and the bottle's on a poodle eating noodles, they call this a muddle puddle tweetle poodle beetle noodle bottle paddle battle." The moral is simple: Avoiding writing like a tweetle beetle.

Revision:

Defendant filed its requests for pretrial identification of documents.

Punctuating for Clarity

The rules of punctuation are not complicated. When we hear a lawyer say that she does not have a firm grasp of the rules governing semicolons, for example, we take that to mean that she has never bothered to spend the 45 minutes it would take to learn them—30 minutes to get to a bookstore or library (any one will do), 5 minutes to find the right book, and 10 minutes to actually learn the rules.

The only tricky part about learning the rules is that occasionally one changes or, at least, is misconstrued by so many people for so long that it creates a dilemma for those who try to obey it. Two minor changes seem to be occurring now:

(1) When you write "the cow, the cat, and the goat," do you need the comma after "cat"? In other words, when you punctuate a series of more than two items, do you need a comma after the next-to-last? Most stylebooks say "yes." Their theory is that the comma sometimes provides a helpful signal about the structure of the series, especially when the list is long or when one of the items in the list includes an "and." That being the case, for the sake of consistency you should always use the comma. Others argue, however, that the comma serves the same function as "and," so you do not need both. We side with the stylebooks, because we think the criterion of clarity is paramount. But many people, and many newspapers and magazines, now omit that comma. In fact, so many have omitted it for so long that some people are now convinced that it is unarguably wrong.

What then should you do? If you are in a position to follow your own judgment, choose the option that makes the most sense to you and stick with it. If you are governed by an institutional stylebook, or by the preferences of those for whom you write, then you may have to conform to the custom of the place.

There is a third alternative, of course, if you are willing to dispense with consistency and rely on common sense instead. Use the comma when it is necessary for clarity, and omit it otherwise. In fact, this solution makes the most sense to us. But the principle of consistency is so ingrained in matters of punctuation that we are in a minority. In this book, as you may have noticed, we always use the comma.

(2) When you write "on March 9, 1991, the shareholder . . . ," do you need the comma after the year? Again, stylebooks say "yes." The year is, in effect, a parenthetical insertion, and the rules say that a parenthetical needs punctuation on both sides. But many people leave out the comma, for the same reason that they leave out the comma in the situation we just discussed: The sentence remains clear without it, whatever the rules say. And, once again, this has gone on for so long that some people believe there is a rule against using the comma after a year.

What should you do? We suggest using the comma. You can always quote authority to back you up, while your opponent probably cannot.

This discussion has had an ulterior motive. There are two reasons for worrying about the rules of punctuation. The first is sociological: What will people think of you if you make mistakes? The dilemmas we just discussed are primarily sociological, and we hope that seeing them from that perspective will help you to regard all arguments about punctuation more rationally.

The second reason for worrying about punctuation is clarity. Hence:

❖   **PUNCTUATION PRINCIPLE 1**   ❖

Punctuation should help the reader understand the sentence.

This basic proposition is the foundation for two other principles:

❖   **PUNCTUATION PRINCIPLE 2**   ❖

*Punctuation should mark the
sentence's grammatical structure.*

Most of the rules of punctuation serve this end. For example, why must you punctuate at the close as well as the opening of a parenthetical phrase? Because the closing punctuation shows the reader where the phrase ends. Why must you put a comma after a phrase that begins the sentence? Because it shows where the phrase ends and the rest of the sentence begins.

This principle should also guide you when there is no rule. Does the punctuation show where clauses and phrases begin and end, and thus help to signal the sentence's structure? If so, use the punctuation.*

Finally, the principle applies when you have a choice among types of punctuation—between a comma and a dash, for example, or between a pair of commas and a pair of parentheses. Occasionally, in a complicated sentence, you may need to turn to dashes or parentheses because they more clearly separate words from the rest of the sentence.

In addition to clarifying a sentence's structure, punctuation can serve a second purpose.

❖   **PUNCTUATION PRINCIPLE 3**   ❖

*Punctuation can help give appropriate
emphasis to information within a sentence.*

Parentheses, for example, signal that the information in them is relatively unimportant. A dash, in contrast, gives emphasis to what follows it.

---

* We have used this principle to resolve, at least in this book, a debate raging among copyeditors and proofreaders: Should you capitalize the first letter following a colon? We capitalize if the colon is followed by a complete sentence, but not otherwise. In other words, we use capitalization to signal the kind of grammatical structure that the colon introduces. One could also argue that the colon most resembles a semicolon, and therefore should never be followed by a capital—a result we also accept as sensible.

CHAPTER **8**

Style: From Clarity
to Grace and Character

TO THIS POINT, we have been describing principles and techniques that make for clear prose. But prose can be effective, in this workmanlike sense, and still be pedestrian. As a lawyer gains skill as a writer, clarity alone should not be enough to satisfy her. Her writing should also begin to show some grace and character—in other words, some style. This does not mean that her prose should sing and dance in a way that calls attention to itself. In legal writing, at least, the style should serve the content, not the writer's ego. More specifically, it should have two goals: to encourage the reader to stay alert and pay attention, and to persuade her to respect and trust the writer. We will call the first goal "grace" and the second "character."

❖   **STYLE PRINCIPLE 1**   ❖

*To keep a reader alert, good writing relies
on structure, not on flashy adornments.*

Amateur writers often think that "style" consists of fancy words, striking metaphors, and an occasional piece of humor. They are wrong. Even if the words are well-chosen, the metaphors original, and the humor good, these adornments are dangerous because they draw attention away from the content of the writing to the words themselves. Writers who rely on these devices ultimately distract rather than please. Never use a word simply because you think it is unusual or striking: Use the most accurate word. If it is also an unusual word, so be it.* We also suggest that you almost never try to be funny—and absolutely never try to be funny at someone else's expense.

Metaphors, on the other hand, can help to make a point memorable. For example:

> The context of this statute is acrid with the smell of threatened impeachment.

Morrison v. Olson, 487 U.S. 654, 702 (1988) (Scalia, J., dissenting).

But writers who try too hard to use metaphors end up with far-fetched or awkward ones:

> Appellants themselves issued the invitations to dance in the federal ballroom, they chose their dancing partners, and at their own request they were assigned a federal judge as their choreographer. Now that the dance is over, appellants find themselves unhappy with the judging of the contest.

The problem here is not only that the metaphor draws too much attention to itself. It is also incoherent: the appellants' dance is a formal ball, and a choreographed show, and a dance contest—simultaneously. Do not reach for a metaphor that does not fit naturally.

As with many questions of style, however, tastes vary. One of the authors of this book offered the metaphor below as a bad example; the other liked it. The right judgment is probably that it would work in some situations (for example, when you want to bring novelty to an overfamiliar subject), but not in others (for example, when you are dealing with a life-and-death issue) that you want to treat with absolute gravity. Judge for yourself:

> Like a thunderstorm on a sultry Southern summer afternoon, the recent spate of contentious articles on the meaning of equality has been loud but inconsequential, cooling the academic air but leaving the legal landscape unchanged.

To give their prose vitality, professional writers rely much less on adornment—including good metaphors—than on two other techniques: syn-

---

* For a sophisticated audience, we see no need to avoid useful words just because they are unusual. This book includes a few of these words ("solipsist" and "syntax," for example). They convey a precise meaning, and the language would be poorer without them.

tactical variety and brevity. With these methods, a writer can create a current of energy that seems natural, not the result of self-conscious pyrotechnics.

❖   **Style Technique 1A**   ❖

Use syntax to create variety.

The artful use of syntax leads not only to well-crafted individual sentences, as we saw in Chapter 5, but also to an invigorating variety of rhythm in a sequence of sentences. In expository writing, readers are seldom conscious of rhythm because their attention is focused on content. But the rhythm affects them nevertheless. Most important, it can encourage them to pay attention. In writing, as in most other things, variety keeps us alert, monotony puts us to sleep.

How can you create variety in a sequence of sentences?

An easy first step is to vary their length. More complexly, vary their internal structure in three ways. First, create pauses of slightly different lengths by using different kinds of punctuation: A dash slows a reader down a little more than a semicolon, which in turn creates a longer pause than a comma. Second, and more important, vary the number of words between the pauses. Finally, vary the complexity of the syntax. The more complex it is, the more it will rely on subordinate clauses and phrases that interrupt the sentence's flow. Here is an example (used earlier for other purposes) of these methods at work:

> We must take September 15 as the culminating date. On this day the Luftwaffe, after two heavy attacks on the 14th, made its greatest concentrated effort in a resumed attack on London.
>
> It was one of the decisive battles of the war, and, like the Battle of Waterloo, it was on a Sunday. I was at Chequers. I had already on several occasions visited the headquarters of Number 11 fighter Group in order to witness the conduct of an air battle, when not much happened. However, the weather on this day seemed suitable to the enemy and accordingly I drove over to Uxbridge and arrived at the Group Headquarters. . . .
>
> Winston Churchill, *History of the Second World War*

The variation in sentence length is obvious. But look also at the variation in syntax between the second and third sentences, on the one hand, and the fifth and sixth. In the former, as we pointed out before, Churchill goes out of his way to interrupt the sentences: Notice the delay between the second sentence's subject and verb and, in the third sentence, the choppy rhythm in the middle. In the fifth and sixth sentences, he does the opposite. In the fifth, the only internal punctuation comes near the end. There, instead of interrupting the sentence dramatically, it prepares for an ending that is anticlimactic in structure as well as content. In the sixth, in order to pull us quickly through the sentence, he allows himself a casual syntax, built around two "and's," that high school English teachers warn against.

The effect is not only to vary the rhythm enough to keep us awake—he first builds up drama and then relaxes the tension, using his syntax to underline what he describes. A superb job, and superbly unobtrusive.

Can you use these techniques in legal writing without being accused of literary affectations? Of course. The conventions will limit the range of effects you create because they require that your style not draw attention to itself. But there is still room for ingenuity. Consider the variety of sentence structures in the relatively plain style of this example:

> Second, the bank itself may become the focus of a criminal investigation. As a general proposition under federal law, a corporation can be held liable for crimes committed by its employees if they are acting within the scope of their employment and if they intend to benefit the corporation. [Citation] Thus, if some lower-level employee proves to have knowingly facilitated a drug dealer's money laundering, the bank is exposed to a criminal prosecution. Worse yet, in recent years corporate criminal liability has been expanded through the doctrine of "collective knowledge." This doctrine holds that a bank's knowledge may be deemed to be the sum of the knowledge of all its employees—regardless of whether any one employee knows enough to infer that a crime is being committed. [Citation] As a result, the bank faces another risk. If the government digs far enough, it may find several employees whose collective knowledge could have alerted the bank that wrongdoing was afoot.

Also note Example 1 on page 8–8.

Remember, though, that the purpose of variety is not simply to keep the reader awake. It is also a means of emphasizing a point. A final example, involving paragraphs rather than sentences, comes from this book itself. Reread the first three paragraphs of the Introduction. The second is a short and rather unusual one. Its two sentences logically belong elsewhere: The first is the concluding thought of the first paragraph and the second is the opening idea of the next paragraph. In other words, we could have written—and, in fact, did originally write—the first page with only two paragraphs, the first ending with "of these methods" and the second beginning with "But its approach . . . ."

Instead, we decided to give these two sentences additional emphasis, and draw the themes on the first page together more dramatically, by pulling these sentences out of their logical home and into a better psychological—and stylistic—one.

❖ **Style Technique 1B** ❖

Be brief.

The second quality of "grace" is brevity. This does not mean that every sentence should be under twelve words long and every argument compressed into shorthand. It means that you should rely more on short sentences than long ones, use no more (and no fancier) words than clarity and completeness require, and refrain from repeating each point in the mistaken belief that you are driving it home.

❖ **STYLE PRINCIPLE 2** ❖

Good writing exhibits character—that is, an appropriate professional persona.

Every time you write, you do more than communicate information. You also reveal a group of attitudes, some that arise from the circumstances of your work and audience, others that are rooted in your personal and professional character. No matter how restrained and impersonal your prose, it expresses what Aristotle calls *ethos*, an image of your character that affects the audience's response. This revelation is unavoidable. The question is not whether you can make your prose anonymous (you can't, and the attempt will produce an atrocious form of bureaucratese), but whether you can become conscious of the attitudes expressed through your writing so that you can control them.

Some of these attitudes emerge from your writing's content: Does it demonstrate the honesty, fairness, thoroughness, and intelligence that establish your credibility? Some emerge from the organizational techniques discussed earlier in this book. Are you taking care to shape your writing to suit the reader, not yourself? Are you in firm control of your organization, or simply piling up paragraphs more-or-less coherently?

These aspects of *ethos* are fairly easy to recognize, once we look for them. A sense of character also emerges, however, from the details of our style, the words we choose, and the shape we give to our sentences—as the young lawyer with the modern vocabulary discovered (see page 7–4).

❖　**Style Technique　2A**　❖

Choose diction and syntax to suit your persona.

Compared to speaking, writing offers fewer opportunities to manifest character through style. A speaker can send out stylistic signals through several channels at once: dress, gesture and body language, tone of voice, the contact her eyes make with the audience. A writer, however, is limited to diction and syntax. Nevertheless, skillful writers can accomplish almost as much with these tools alone. Here are two writers setting out to create an *ethos* for their narrators quickly and pungently in a novel's first paragraph. Look at the diction and syntax, not just the content:

> You don't know about me without you have read a book by the name of *The Adventures of Tom Sawyer*, but that ain't no matter. That book was made by Mr. Mark Twain and he told the truth, mainly. There was things which he stretched, but mainly he told the truth. That is nothing. I never seen anybody but lied one time or another. . . .
>
> Mark Twain, *The Adventures of Huckleberry Finn*

> I am an American, Chicago born—Chicago, that somber city—and go at things as I taught myself, free-style, and will make the record in my own way: first to knock, first admitted; sometimes an innocent knock, sometimes a not so innocent. But a man's character is his fate, says Heraclitus, and in the end there isn't any way to disguise the nature of the knocks by acoustical work on the door or gloving the knuckles.
>
> Saul Bellow, *The Adventures of Augie Marsh*

Unlike novelists and essayists, of course, lawyers generally do not want to give their prose the strong flavor of a personality. They prefer to submerge their idiosyncrasies in their professional roles. But even the most restrained legal prose reveals something of your professional character, and perhaps your personal character as well. Quite different characters emerge from these two judicial opinions:

EXAMPLE 1

In this malpractice lawsuit, the issue on appeal is whether the trial judge properly granted the defendant's motion for summary judgment.

The defendants filed a motion to dismiss because the complaint failed to state a claim on which relief could be granted. They then filed four affidavits to support their motion and moved the court to treat the motion as one for summary judgment. The court agreed, and allowed the plaintiffs 30 days to file counteraffidavits. When the plaintiffs did not file, the trial judge granted summary judgment against them.

EXAMPLE 2

This case comes before the court on the third intermediate accounting of the trust under the will of Jane F. Smith. On a prior accounting, the West Carolina Supreme Court held that a provision in a will leaving property to "issue" of another is presumed not to include the adopted child of the daughter of the testatrix. We are now asked to reconsider the question based on subsequent changes in the decisional law of this State. The case raises a substantial, if not altogether novel, question of the duty of a court to enforce a prior holding, the legal reasoning of which has been undermined by later rulings.

In the first example, the judge prefers short and simply constructed sentences, and is not afraid of language that approaches the informal ("The court agreed . . . ."). We sense a plain-spoken character who disdains sophisticated airs. In the second example, we see a judge who appreciates the traditions that elevate the law above the street. In her diction, she sometimes chooses the more formal of two available words ("subsequent" rather than "later"), and once employs a turn of phrase that we could not use in conversation without sounding pedantic ("the legal reasoning of which . . ."). In her syntax, she prefers long and relatively complex sentences.

As these examples show, prose reveals an *ethos* even when it does not flaunt a personality. You cannot hide behind your writing. Yet it takes a self-conscious effort to recognize and control the attitudes your writing conveys—unless you are one of the lucky few who grew up writing so much that their written style has long since molded itself to their mind's shape. The opposite extreme is more common. Most of us know someone who speaks with Will Rogers' directness, but writes with the pretentiousness of Dickens' Micawber announcing that his daughter is learning to be a milkmaid: "My eldest daughter attends at five every morning in a neighboring establishment, to acquire the process of milking cows." When a writer's character and style diverge like that, two things have usually gone wrong: She has failed to consider the attitudes she wants her writing to embody and, as a result, she has adopted indiscriminately the style of other legal writing she has read since the first day of law school.

To avoid any misunderstanding, we emphasize one point already made in passing. While your writing cannot help but project character, this does not mean that you should try to become a "character" by creating a style so unusual that it draws attention as much to you as to its content. Save this for your memoirs. In legal writing, the most effective character often has the same qualities as pellucid mountain air: it seems to make everything it touches stand out more clearly, while being invisible itself. The best style is sometimes the plainest, because it shows that you are focused on your subject matter and have reduced it to its essentials. (See Example 1 below.)

Even when you are trying to create a distinctive style, the result should be that readers notice an unusual flavor that makes the content more memorable—not that they are awestruck by your flights of fancy. As we said earlier, the way to create this flavor is through careful manipulation of syntax. (See Example 2.)

EXAMPLE 1

By this motion, Smith seeks dismissal of the only claim in Jones' complaint that survived the jury's verdict. The complaint recited six causes of action. One, breach of contract, was dismissed by Jones prior to trial. Another, tortious interference with business relations, was dismissed by this Court at the close of Jones' case. Of the four claims that went to the jury, the jury found in Smith's favor on three: fraud and breach of express and implied warranties of title. The only claim on which the jury found in Jones' favor was breach of the implied warranty of merchantability.

In this memorandum, we shall demonstrate that judgment should be entered for Smith on this claim. Three reasons compel this conclusion. First, although the jury found that the warranty of merchantability had been breached, Jones introduced no evidence on the subject of whether "The Orchard" would be deemed marketable under the standards of the international art market. The jury received no guidance as to the standards of merchantability for Old Master paintings, and its verdict was thus based on sheer speculation.

Second, the alleged breach of warranty occurred with respect to goods that were never sold to Jones. Jones was therefore left to argue that Smith had anticipatorily repudiated its contract within the meaning of Section 2-609 of the Uniform Commercial Code. Before there can be a finding of anticipatory repudiation, a party must make a written demand for adequate assurance of due performance. Jones made no such written demand.

Third, ...

EXAMPLE 2

The conservatee, Robert Jones, sold his business at the end of 1982. It was failing, and his family and friends realized that his memory and ability to handle complex issues were also failing. After the sale, Jones became depressed. Then began a slow and steady deterioration of his condition, leading finally to a diagnosis of Alzheimer's disease. In April of 1987, when he was 72 years old, this petition was filed.

❖ **Style Technique 2B** ❖

Choose and maintain an appropriate level of formality.

Among the attitudes you should consider, the most obvious is the degree of formality you prefer. Between the extremes of pomposity and slanginess, you have a range of choices. As the examples above illustrated, those choices should influence both the kinds of words you use and the kinds of sentences you shape. A difference in diction is the easiest to spot and to control. Here, for example, are several versions of the same sentence, with only the diction changing:

> Prior to the plaintiff's purchase of the automobile, defendant's salesman provided him with false information about its previous owner.

> Before the plaintiff bought the automobile, the defendant's salesman provided him with false information about its previous owner.

> Before the plaintiff bought the car, the defendant's salesman gave him false information about its last owner.

> The sucker got stuck with the lemon, because the salesman fed him some **** about the guy who got rid of it.

Except for the last, which may be the most accurate, a legal writer could choose any of these versions.

Our own search for an appropriate diction has been more difficult than we expected. The book's final style represents a compromise between the tastes of its two authors. One, the other feared, was too fond of loose colloquialisms, a tendency he tried to defend on populist grounds. The second, so the first thought, showed a elitist distaste for one-syllable words, a tendency he defended by arguing that the book was, after all, written for lawyers. In the search for a middle ground, we decided to adopt a style that would suit a brief or a business letter to a stranger, so that we would not take stylistic liberties that our readers could not take in their professional writing. As a result, when we edited the manuscript we elevated the diction of some relatively colloquial sentences. "Sending it back," for example, became "returning it," "a lot better" became "much better," and we eliminated contractions such as "don't" and "we're." But we were aiming for the effect of a twentieth-century business suit, not nineteenth-century top hat and tails. As a result, we also revised some sentences to sound less formal. In the book's second paragraph, for example, the second sentence once read:

> Its approach is sufficiently unusual, however, to require some explanation.

This became:

> But its approach is unusual enough to warrant some explanation.

The lesson of our struggle, we decided, is that legal writers find it difficult to choose an appropriate level of formality because legal writing does not reflect a consensus about what that level should be. Each lawyer is faced, therefore, with an individual decision about the persona she wants her writing to present. And, unless you think about choices such as those represented by the sentences on the previous page, your style is unlikely to suit the persona you prefer.

Once you have made your choice, take care to keep your diction consistent throughout a document. Do not mix styles:

> Upon arriving at the cottage, the officers knocked on the door, but received no answer. They yelled "police," but again received no answer. They heard a "faint shuffling sound, but no loud noises" from inside, whereupon they kicked the door open and handcuffed the Defendant.

This paragraph produces the effect of someone wearing lawyers' pinstripes above the waist and cut-off blue jeans below. "Upon entering" and "yelled" are each appropriate in some contexts, but not in the same one. And the formality of "whereupon" does not belong in the same sentence as, much less next to, the simplicity of "they kicked the door open . . . ."

```
❖    Style Technique  2C    ❖
           Avoid jargon.
```

Like all professions, the law uses words to which it has given a specific definition, and which cannot be easily translated into layman's language. What plain-English alternative is there to *habeas corpus*? In addition to these necessary terms of art, however, the law has grown attached to other words—"said," as in "said document," for example—that serve as the profession's caste mark, signalling a lawyer at work. Unlike terms such as *habeas corpus*, these words have no practical use: What they mean can be translated easily into plain English. They are used not because they are precise, but because they make a lawyer feel like a lawyer when she writes. In addition to "said," the most frequent offenders are:

❖ "Such," as in ". . . the agreement to which we have referred. Such agreement . . . ." Use "this" instead.

❖ "Herein," "hereafter," "aforementioned," etc.

❖ "Prior to" and "subsequent to," instead of "before" and "after."

❖ Ritual phraseology intended, presumably, to surround an occasion with an aura of impressiveness ("comes now before the court," "whereas," etc.).

❖ Latin words that, unlike "*habeas corpus*," have no precise legal meaning ("*inter alia*").

If you use this kind of jargon, you pay a heavy price. It does more than make your prose affected and clumsy. It also conveys an unfortunate *ethos*, because it suggests that you rely too much on the superficial aspects of your language to demonstrate your professionalism. In addition, if your audience consists of non-lawyers, this jargon gives the impression that you are going out of your way to emphasize the difference between you and them.

❖ **STYLE PRINCIPLE 3** ❖

*Do not denigrate your opponents or any-
one else (except, sometimes, to their faces).*

Many lawyers are combative by nature, and their feistiness sometimes spills onto paper in unfortunate ways. Even when you are writing to issue an ultimatum or respond to an outrageous demand, avoid a tone that is unnecessarily argumentative or abrasive. Insulting your opponent may make you feel better, but it does nothing else for you—and, if you want your audience to do something, an abrasive tone may work against you.

Litigators in particular must learn to walk the fine line between a strong argument and a table-thumping, mud-throwing one. On paper, at least, the most persuasive advocates are the ones who rely on calm—but firmly stated—reasoning. They do not launch personal attacks against their opponents, or describe their opponents' arguments as stupid (even when they are), or, in appellate briefs, criticize the competence of the court below. Even if these attacks are based on undeniable, overwhelming evidence, they will damage your credibility and distract from your argument. The judge will probably think that you exaggerate or, at the least, have bad manners. At worst, she will begin to look for redeeming qualities in the person you attack. At best, she will form her own judgment—and she will feel more comfortable with that judgment if you have not tried to force it on her. The art of written persuasion is in finding a way to lead your readers to the conclusion you want them to reach so that they are happy to reach it. They will not be happy if you are implicitly asking them to join you in slinging mud at your opponent.

CHAPTER 9

Wielding a Sharp Red Pencil: Editing Yourself and Others

EDITING IS THE STAGE at which we take full control of our writing. In the throes of a first draft, what control we have is mostly intuitive, even if we outlined first. When we edit, we can apply some conscious, focused methods of diagnosis and treatment. As a result, editing can have dramatic results even when we are pressed for time—if we know how to edit effectively.

The second section of this Chapter suggests four basic principles, accompanied by some techniques, for approaching the editing process systematically, and hence more successfully. First, though, we want to pause for a moment over the question of why good editing is so important not just to your own writing, but to the legal profession itself.

Editing as a Collegial Activity

Many lawyers, perhaps most, work in firms or in corporate or governmental legal departments. In these institutions, the more senior lawyers spend a lot of time editing the writing of their juniors, especially now that word processing allows drafts to be retyped so rapidly. One aim of this editing, of course, is to improve the draft. In the long run, another aim should be to improve the general quality of writing in the group. Senior lawyers need to use their editorial skill so that it aids the development of the writers they supervise. But most are better at fixing a draft themselves than at showing the writer how to do better the next time. The result is wasted time and frustration on both sides.

One sign of this problem is that senior lawyers are likely to have widely varying, idiosyncratic editing styles. One will be a line-by-line niggler, another will attack viciously with a red pen and biting criticism, another will send a draft back with a few general comments. Moreover, each will probably stick with the same editorial style for all occasions, suggesting that it is a reflex rather than a tool employed for a specific end. Ideally, in contrast, each senior lawyer should bring several possible approaches to an edit so that she can choose the one best suited to the occasion—and every senior lawyer should rely on roughly the same range of approaches. As a result, when a junior lawyer receives different types of edits, the difference would reflect the types of problems that different editors saw in her draft, not just their idiosyncratic styles.

Before we offer specific advice about editing, here are some examples of typical editing styles. Aside from the first—which the cynical among you might call the "standard partner feedback" style—they all have aspects that will be effective in some situations but not in others.

EXAMPLE 1

14

NO

That case, however, has been severally criticized if not virtually overruled. <u>See</u> <u>Babkanic v. General Administration of Civil Aviation of the Peoples' Republic of China</u>, 822 F.2d 11 (2d Cir. 1987). In fact at this point, <u>In Re Rio Grande Transport</u> is difficult to reconcile with the holding in <u>Martin</u>. <u>See</u> <u>Close v. American Airlines, Inc.</u>, 587 F. Supp. 1062, 1065 (S.D.N.Y. 1984). To allow a United States corporation suffering financial loss in the United States due to events occurring outside the United States to enjoy greater access to the courts than an American citizen injured abroad would seem somewhat anomalous. <u>Id</u>. Therefore, the rule applicable to American citizens injured abroad should also apply to United States corporations injured abroad. The financial loss suffered by a United States corporation in this country as a result of events occurring outside the United States, therefore, cannot be deemed to create a "direct effect in the United States" for purposes of the FSIA.

If a United States corporation cannot recover for such loss, <u>a fortiorari</u>, a foreign corporation cannot recover for similar losses. As a result, whatever financial loss Akropan a foreign corporation, may have suffered in the United States as a result of the explosion in the port of Skikda, Algeria, cannot, as a matter of law, be deemed to amount to a "direct effect in the United States". Therefore, Defendants are immune from this Court's jurisdiction and

Draft: 10/05/88   NYCCC202   Document No. 2449g

15

Akropan's third party complaint should be dismissed.

C.   The Claim Against NAFTEC should be dismissed
        for lack of In personam Jurisdiction   -

The complaint against NAFTEC should be dismissed for lack of in personam jurisdiction . Under the FSIA, a court may exercise personal jurisdiction over a foreign state if that state or its agency or instrumentality has sufficient " minimum contacts" with the United States. See Texas Trading Milling Corp. v. Federal Republic of Nigeria, 647 F.2d 300, 308 (2d Cir. 1981). Courts must examine: 1) the extent to which defendant availed itself of the privileges of American law, 2) the extent to which the litigation in the United States would be forseeable to the defendant, 3) the inconvenience to the defendant of litigating in the United States, and 4) the countervailing interest of the United States in hearing the suit. Id. citing World-Wide Volkswagen Corp. v. Woodson, 444 U.S. 286, 292, 297 (1980). The standard under the FSIA calls for evidence of continuous and systematic activities in the United States. Gemini Shipping, Inc. v. Foreign Trade Organization For Chemicals And Foodstuffs, 496 F. Supp. 256 (S.D.N.Y. 1980); see Crimson Semiconductor Inc., v. Electronum, 629 F. Supp. 903, 907-08 (S.D.N.Y. 1986). A foreign state's occasional commercial contacts with the United States will not suffice to establish minimum contacts for the purpose of in personam jurisdiction. See Paterson, Zochonis (U.K.) LTD. v. Compania

NO

Draft: 10/05/88   NYCCC202   Document No. 2449g

16

United Arrow, S.A., 493 F. Supp. 621 (S.D.N.Y. 1980).

Both defendants had substantial and continuous contacts with the United States. In that case, defendant ; a state-owned trading company, had done business with the plaintiff and other United States corporations for a decade. Crimson Semiconductor Inc., v. Electronum, 629 F. Supp. 903, 907-08 (S.D.N.Y. 1986). Defendant delivered its products to the United States, engaged consultants to monitor demand in this country, advertised here, made and received payment through United States banks and negotiated, directly or through its agents, distribution agreements in the United States. Defendant had even initiated attachment proceedings against the plaintiff in United States courts. 629 F. Supp. at 907-08. The Court found that defendant availed itself of the benefits of American law through its exploitation of United States markets and its use of United States courts. Defendant's delivery of goods to the United States made litigation here foreseeable and not overly inconvenient.

In this case, NAFTEC's activities in the United States are non-existent. Therefore, the court may not in accordance with due process exercise personal jurisdiction over NAFTEC. NAFTEC s business is strictly domestic. NAFTEC refines all Algerian oil but distributes the oil only in Algeria. NAFTEC does not conduct any business in or with the United States or maintain an office in this country. It does

NO

Draft: 10/05/88   NYCCC202   Document No. 2449g

17

not maintain a mailing address, post office box or telephone
in the United States. NAFTEC does not advertise, solicit
business, or send its agents or employees to this country.
NAPTEC had no reason to believe that it would now be the
target of litigation instituted in the Southern District of
New York by a panamanian corporation with whom it has no
contractual or other relationship.

NAFTEC has not availed itself of the privileges of
American law and litigation in New York was absolutely
unforseeable. To force NAFTEC to litigate Akropan's claim in
New York would be extremely inconvenient since NAFTEC has no
presence in the United States. Finally, the United States
has no interest in hearing a suit between a panamanian
corporation and an Algerian company arising out of an
accident which took place in Algeria on a Bahamian Tanker
loading Algerian oil destined for Northern Europe. NAFTEC
does not have sufficient "minimum contacts" with the United
States to justify this Court in exercising personal
jurisdiction over it. Any exercise of personal jurisdiction
over NAFTEC would violate all traditional notions of fair
play and justice. See International Shoe, _____.

REWRITE

Draft: 10/05/88   NYCCC202   Document No. 2449g

Examples 2 and 3 are the same pages edited by two partners. Example 2 makes changes to sentences, but does not provide any general comments on approach or organization.

EXAMPLE 2

IN THE

SUPREME COURT OF THE UNITED STATES

OCTOBER TERM, 1984

No. 83-1569

MITSUBISHI MOTORS CORPORATION,

Petitioner,

- v. -

SOLER CHRYSLER-PLYMOUTH, INC.,

Respondent.

On Writ of Certiorari to the United States
Court of Appeals for the First Circuit

MOTION FOR LEAVE
TO FILE BRIEF
OF AMICUS CURIAE

Pursuant to Rule 36.3 of the Rules of this Court, the American Arbitration Association (hereinafter "AAA" or the "Association") hereby respectfully moves for leave to file the annexed brief amicus curiae. The written consent of petitioner has been obtained. The consent of respondent was requested but refused.

2

The AAA is an educational, membership organization founded in 1926 and incorporated under the Not-for-Profit Corporation Law of the State of New York. The Association is dedicated to the ~~dissemination of~~ knowledge throughout the United States and other countries regarding arbitration as an alternative ~~mechanism for the resolution of~~ disputes. The AAA does not act as an arbitrator of disputes; rather, it provides impartial rules, procedures, and administrative assistance to parties desiring to use its neutral facilities.

disseminating

means for resolving

In This ~~is the first~~ case, ~~in which~~ this Court has been asked to determine the arbitrability of a transnational commercial dispute that implicates United States antitrust laws. The AAA ~~believes that it~~ can present to this Court a broader perspective than the one presented by the parties. By virtue of its half-century long experience in private dispute resolution and its many years of experience with the international arbitral process, the AAA is uniquely qualified to address the issues now before the Court as they relate to international arbitration agreements.

for the first time

In the past year, approximately 40,000 arbitrations -- were conducted under the auspices of the AAA, many of which were international in nature. The AAA also maintains cooperative, reciprocal arrangements with numerous arbitration associations around the world, including the Japan Commercial Arbitration Association, the London Court of Arbitration, the Hungarian Chamber of Commerce, Associazione Italiana Per L'Arbitrato, the Korean Commercial Arbitration Association and the Regional Centre for Arbitration at Cairo.

Can we specify # of intern'l arbs. ?

3

The AAA was in the forefront of organizations recommending accession by the United States to the United Nations Convention on the Recognition and Enforcement of Foreign Arbitral Awards, 21 U.S.T. 2517, T.I.A.S. No. 6997, 330 U.N.T.S. 38 (1958). The Convention, which was ratified by the United States in 1970, provides among other things for prompt and effective enforcement of voluntary international agreements to arbitrate. At the request of the State Department, the Association convened a committee of international arbitration experts to draft proposed implementing legislation. The AAA's proposal formed the basis for what is now Chapter 2 of the United States Arbitration Act, 9 U.S.C. §§ 201-08 (1982).

The AAA has no direct interest in the administration of the ~~international~~ arbitration between the parties. Nor ~~has the AAA~~ *does it have* any interest in the underlying merits of the dispute. The Association's concern here is in having our judicial system reconfirm the fundamental importance and certainty of arbitration in international commercial relationships.

WHEREFORE, the American Arbitration Association respectfully moves this Court for leave to file the annexed brief as <u>amicus curiae</u> in support of Petitioner.

Respectfully submitted,

<u>Attorneys for Amicus Curiae</u>
<u>American Arbitration Association</u>

December 10, 1984

Example 3 illustrates the style of the "marginal commenter." The editor provides advice, but does not make changes in the text.

EXAMPLE 3

JTM
12/2

No. 83-1569

IN THE

SUPREME COURT OF THE UNITED STATES

OCTOBER TERM, 1984

MITSUBISHI MOTORS CORPORATION,

Petitioner,

- v. -

SOLER CHRYSLER-PLYMOUTH, INC.,

Respondent.

On Writ of Certiorari to the United States
Court of Appeals for the First Circuit

MOTION FOR LEAVE TO FILE BRIEF OF
AMICUS CURIAE AND BRIEF OF THE
AMERICAN ARBITRATION ASSOCIATION AS
AMICUS CURIAE IN SUPPORT OF PETITIONER

Of Counsel:

Attorneys for Amicus Curiae
American Arbitration Association

December 10, 1984

[Handwritten marginal notes, left:] Need more authorities, particularly secondary sources.

)"Safety valve" of article V argument not squarely presented - I think it should be.

[Handwritten marginal notes, right:]
1) I like structure and think tinkering should be kept to a minimum

2) 1st argument is not crystal clear - we need to conclude that U.S. legislation creating an anti-trust exception is required and does not exist.

3) Relationship of 2d argument to 1st needs clarification - even if legislation is not required (i.e., courts can create exceptions) court should not create exception here for policy reasons

IN THE

SUPREME COURT OF THE UNITED STATES

OCTOBER TERM, 1984

No. 83-1569

_____

MITSUBISHI MOTORS CORPORATION,

Petitioner,

- v. -

SOLER CHRYSLER-PLYMOUTH, INC.,

Respondent.

_____

_____

On Writ of Certiorari to the United States
Court of Appeals for the First Circuit

_____

_____

MOTION FOR LEAVE
TO FILE BRIEF
OF AMICUS CURIAE

_____

Pursuant to Rule 36.3 of the Rules of this Court, the
American Arbitration Association (hereinafter "AAA" or the
"Association") hereby respectfully moves for leave to file the
annexed brief amicus curiae. The written consent of petitioner
has been obtained. The consent of respondent was requested but
refused.

2

The AAA is an educational, membership organization founded in 1926 and incorporated under the Not-for-Profit Corporation Law of the State of New York. The Association is dedicated to the dissemination of knowledge throughout the United States and other countries regarding arbitration as an alternative mechanism for the resolution of disputes. The AAA does not act as an arbitrator of disputes; rather, it provides impartial rules, procedures, and administrative assistance to parties desiring to use its neutral facilities.

This is the first case in which this Court has been asked to determine the arbitrability of a transnational commercial dispute that implicates United States antitrust laws. The AAA believes that it can present to this Court a broader perspective than the one presented by the parties. By virtue of its half-century long experience in private dispute resolution and its many years of experience with the international arbitral process, the AAA is uniquely qualified to address issues before the Court as they relate to international arbitration agreements.

In the past year, approximately 40,000 arbitrations were conducted under the auspices of the AAA, many of which were international in nature. The AAA also maintains cooperative, reciprocal arrangements with numerous arbitration associations around the world, including the Japan Commercial Arbitration Association, the London Court of Arbitration, the Hungarian Chamber of Commerce, Associazione Italiana Per L'Arbitrato, the Korean Commercial Arbitration Association and the Regional Centre for Arbitration at Cairo.

[handwritten marginalia: "...o we ...ve ...ecifics or ...ternational bitation" — ...rticularly ... trend over ...e]

3

The AAA was in the forefront of organizations recommending accession by the United States to the United Nations Convention on the Recognition and Enforcement of Foreign Arbitral Awards, 21 U.S.T. 2517, T.I.A.S. No. 6997, 330 U.N.T.S. 38 (1958). The Convention, which was ratified by the United States in 1970, provides among other things for prompt and effective enforcement of voluntary international agreements to arbitrate. At the request of the State Department, the Association convened a committee of international arbitration experts to draft proposed implementing legislation. The AAA's *any cites for this?* proposal formed the basis for what is now Chapter 2 of the United States Arbitration Act, 9 U.S.C. §§ 201–08 (1982).

The AAA has no direct interest in the administration of the international arbitration between the parties. Nor has the AAA any interest in the underlying merits of the dispute. The Association's concern here is in having our judicial system reconfirm the fundamental importance and certainty of arbitration in international commercial relationships.

WHEREFORE, the American Arbitration Association respectfully moves this Court for leave to file the annexed brief as <u>amicus curiae</u> in support of Petitioner.

Respectfully submitted,

<u>Attorneys for Amicus Curiae</u>
<u>American Arbitration Association</u>

December 10, 1984

Finally, Example 4 illustrates a good, close edit of an associate's letter that adds an extra dimension not often taught at partner school. Returning the letter covered in red marks, the partner adds the comment: "A few suggestions re: style. Thanks for your help on these matters—you are doing fine!" This comment is significant for two reasons. First, although the partner's edit in fact goes well beyond a few stylistic suggestions, she nevertheless softens the blow by characterizing the edit in this less threatening form. Second, she softens the impact further with her quick thanks and a pat on the back. These comments illustrate a concern for the psychological impact of the edit on the associate, an issue discussed in the next section.

The partner's comment would have been improved even further if she had added another dimension: an explanation of her changes, most of which were intended to make the letter sound less formal and legalistic.

EXAMPLE 4

This agreement extends

VIA HAND DELIVERY

Ms.
Trust Office
Trust Company Bank
Atlanta, Georgia 30303

        Re: Trust Company Bank, ~~as~~ successor Trustee ~~under~~ _u/A_
        ~~Agreement~~ with Peter A.   ᵃ dated July 14,
        1983

Dear Caroline:

        I ~~have~~ enclosed an execution counterpart of _the_ First
Consolidated Amendatory Agreement, dated as of March 31,
1987, ~~by and~~ between John   , Samuel   . Sr. and B. L.
    ., as Purchasers~~, therein~~, and Trust Company Bank as   _u/A_
successor Trustee ~~under Agreement~~ with Peter A.
dated July 14, 1983. ~~which serves to extend~~ the maturity date
of the ~~subject~~ purchase money indebtedness from March 31,
1987 to May 31, 1987. ~~I would appreciate your executing~~ the   _# Please_
Agreement on behalf of Trust Company Bank and affix~~ing~~ the   _execute_
bank seal where ~~provided~~ _indicated_. ~~Upon,~~ execution, ~~I would appreciate~~   _After_
~~your sending~~ _please send_ the Agreement back to me so that I may forward
~~same~~ _it_ to Bob Garrison for execution by the Purchasers.

        I would be pleased to answer any questions or
address any comments you may have regarding the Agreement.

        With best regards.

                        Yours very truly,

_To ⟶_

Enclosure

cc:

J— A few suggestions re: style. Thanks for your help on these matters — you are doing fine.

Principles and Techniques of Good Editing

We turn now to the principles and techniques of editing that are crucial to your skill as a writer.

❖   **EDITING PRINCIPLE 1**   ❖

Good editing requires time.

The greatest cause of mediocre legal writing is that writers do not save enough time for editing. (The second-greatest cause, as we will see below, is that they do not know how to use the time they do have.) This problem has three sources.

First, most writers begin writing too late in the assignment. With a research memo or brief, they want to finish all the research first. As a result, the writing and editing get crammed into too little time. If they were to start writing pieces of the draft earlier, they would find their time allocated more sensibly between research and writing.

Second, most writers do not build time for editing into their schedule for an assignment. Ideally, the schedule should force the writer to put the draft aside for a while so that she can approach it with a fresh eye when she edits. We know that many assignments are too rushed for this scheduling—but fewer than writers claim.

Third, many young lawyers seem to have survived writing assignments in college and law school (with the exception of law review writing) by turning in what were basically first drafts, lightly edited to fix glaring errors. They are unprepared to regard editing as a serious, laborious activity. If you recognize yourself in this description, change your ways. When you do not see much that you can improve in a draft, mistrust your vision.

❖   **EDITING PRINCIPLE 2**   ❖

Good editing is carefully organized.

Assume that your secretary has just returned the draft of a twenty-page memo. It looks crisp and polished. You know better. But you have only two hours to edit before the overnight mail deadline at 8 p.m. Where do you start?

Many people would pick up a pencil, apply it to the first sentence and proceed to the last, fixing whatever problems catch their eye along the way—a typo, a clumsy sentence, an ambiguously phrased conclusion, a misplaced paragraph, a murky explanation of a legal principle. If they are talented editors, they may produce a second draft that is a good deal better than the first. But even the most talented will have improved matters less than they could have.

This method of editing—as instinctive as it is for most of us—has two problems. First, we are trying to handle too many tasks at once: checking for flaws in our analysis, testing the organization, copyediting for stylistic and grammatical problems, and proofreading. We cannot do a good job with all of them at once, especially since they require different types of attention. Trying to copyedit and to fix organization at the same time is like trying to look simultaneously at a window frame and the mountains in the distance.

Second, if we start by diving head first into the swamp of prose in front of us, it is much harder to diagnose the draft's problems. We risk spending too much time tinkering with minor flaws and too little dealing with major, structural problems.

The moral: Good editors are organized editors. Except with short documents, they break the edit into stages.

Being organized is especially important if you are short on time. (It may also feel counterintuitive then, since you are in a hurry.) It is also especially important if you have someone else's draft in front of you and plan to make only the vital improvements yourself, returning it with instructions for a more thorough rewrite. But being organized is important even if you spend several hours on a revision. In this lucky situation, you still need to understand the separate tasks facing you and, at some point, to focus on each of them.

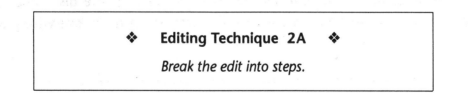

❖   **Editing Technique 2A**   ❖

Break the edit into steps.

Assuming that you are already satisfied with the content, the major stages in an edit coincide with the principal divisions of this book:

1. Editing for your audience. Is the document's tone, length, and basic approach appropriate?
2. Editing for organization (including the content of the introduction, which is usually shortchanged in a first draft).

3. Editing for the coherence of paragraphs and smoothness of transitions between and within them.
4. Editing for the clarity of sentences.
5. Editing for correctness of grammar and punctuation.
6. Proofreading.

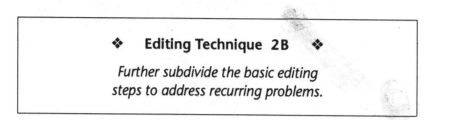

❖ **Editing Technique 2B** ❖

*Further subdivide the basic editing
steps to address recurring problems.*

In a particularly thorough edit, you may want to break some of the above stages into smaller steps, to address specific problems that often give you trouble. As you work on sentences, for example, you could devote one read-through just to untangling overly complex sentences and another to smoothing out transitions among sentences. Aside from its effects on the draft, this technique is one of the best ways to improve your writing in general. By the time you have concentrated on a specific problem through several edits, the problem will appear less often in first drafts because you will be avoiding it as you first put the words down on the page.

Editing never becomes wholly mechanical. You will not go through all of the stages listed in Editing Technique 2A with every document, of course, nor will you always devote a separate revision to each stage. If you had some sleep the night before, you can afford to rely to some degree on free-form intelligence. But most of us should organize the editing process more than we do. In the long run, to be effective we have to develop the discipline to concentrate our efforts and the patience to resist trying to fix everything at once.

❖ **EDITING PRINCIPLE 3** ❖

Good editing anticipates the most likely problems.

Effectiveness as an editor also depends on skill as a diagnostician. As you approach a draft, you should be able to predict many of the problems you will encounter, and therefore to spot them more quickly when they appear.

Luckily, the range of problems you will encounter is smaller than the variety a college writing instructor faces. If the people with whom you work write decent professional prose, none is likely to commit linguistic sins that are at all imaginative, compared to the adventures in prose of college students. As a result, you will see many of the same problems again and again.

Among professional writers, most problems can be traced back to one of two sources:

1. individual bad habits that each of us develops, and
2. inherent difficulties of writing about complex issues.

The inherent difficulties arise because, when we are trying to communicate complex information, most of our energy is expended trying to present it in a roughly logical sequence; we do not have much energy left for working on clarity and persuasiveness. In the first draft, in other words, and perhaps in the second, our job is to do justice to the content. In later drafts, we should do justice to the reader—a job that requires the stylistic and organizational tactics described in the book's earlier chapters. Almost inevitably, for example, a draft will need major surgery to its introduction, and probably to the introductions to its sections. If it draws on much case law, you will probably have to tie each case more clearly to your analysis before discussing it. Transitions will be inadequate. Stylistically, you will have written many clumsily constructed sentences because you were using them simply as rough-and-ready containers for their content.

The techniques in the earlier chapters can be transformed into a checklist of the problems you will see in many drafts. Drawing on them and on your own experience, you should begin to construct your own checklists—one for the problems you can expect in all drafts, another for your own idiosyncrasies.

❖   **EDITING PRINCIPLE 4**   ❖

Good editing requires objectivity and distance.

So far, we have discussed editing as a matter of mechanics. It is also a matter of psychology. But the psychology differs drastically depending upon whether you are editing your own writing or another's.

❖   **Editing Technique 4A**   ❖

*When editing your own writing, act
as if it were written by someone else.*

You must develop the knack of treating your own drafts as if they were the work of a casual acquaintance you do not trust much. This knack is hard to acquire. Your drafts are your own offspring, and a flaw in them may feel like a flaw in yourself. Moreover, most of us learned in school to connect the number of marks a teacher made on a paper with the grade it received. Once you leave school, you may still assume only incompetent writing needs heavy editing.

This assumption is fatal. Good professional writers take it for granted that if they return to a paragraph three times, each time they will find a way to improve it. They also recognize that drafting and editing are separate stages that focus on different (although overlapping) tasks. As a result, professional writers take pride in the outcome of the editing rather than the quality of the first draft.

❖   **Editing Technique 4B**   ❖

*When editing others, recognize
the edit's psychological impact.*

When you edit your own writing, time is the only limitation on how much you do. Given enough time, you should show a draft no mercy. When you edit someone else's writing, you may decide to impose other limits. You may be concerned with the writer's morale or your working relationship, or you may want her to respond actively to the draft's problems rather than just to accept your changes. As a result, instead of making all the changes yourself, you may ask the writer to make some of them. And you may decide to settle for an adequate rather than a brilliant style, because you do not want to drown the writer in red ink. (Or, of course, because you are in no position politically to criticize her style.)

For editing other people's writing, the following two techniques are critical.

> ❖ **Editing Technique 4C** ❖
>
> *Decide in advance how detailed an edit to impose.*

If you are editing someone else's draft, the first step is to decide what kind of editing to do. Are you going to make only the major improvements and, perhaps, give the author instructions for a more thorough revision? Or are you going to revise as thoroughly as if it were your own draft, rewriting everything that can be improved? If the latter, where will you draw the line between matters of professional judgment and matters of personal taste? Are you going to allow the writer her own distinctive style, or will you transform it into your own style?

Many people, even those who do a lot of editing, never ask themselves these questions. As a result, they edit every draft they see in the same way, whether or not it is appropriate. The problem is compounded because lawyers usually edit the writing of subordinates who, being subordinates, are unlikely to tell them that they edit inefficiently.

> ❖ **Editing Technique 4D** ❖
>
> *Whenever possible, use the edit to teach: Explain your changes and allow the author to participate in the exercise.*

Editing other people's writing is tricky because of the sensitivities involved. Ideally, we welcome an intelligent edit, whatever flaws it reveals. In practice, our tolerance has its lapses. When you edit the writing of a subordinate, the other person should feel enlightened, not victimized. This requires, first of all, some self-restraint—which is not to be confused with softheartedness. Be explicit about the draft's problems, but avoid imposing your own tastes on the writer (except when she has drafted a speech or letter that is supposed to carry your flavor). In addition, enlightenment requires the diplomatic use of three tactics:

First, when the reasons for a change are not self-evident, explain them. Because they usually will be self-evident, you should not end up with overflowing margins. In general, you will do enough if you explain a few specific changes in the margins and add a couple of more general notes about the kind of changes you have made.

Second, resist the urge to fix everything yourself. Instead, ask the writer to fix some of it. Otherwise, the same problems may reappear in the next document she writes.

Third, try to create a dialogue with the writer about your changes. The simplest method is to add a few general comments on the first or last page of the draft. Aside from their content—and it may be the most useful part of your edit in improving the author's writing—they show that you are thinking about the writer behind the prose, not just taking a scalpel to an anonymous, sheet-draped patient. If you are editing drafts from someone with whom you will work frequently, take one more step: Sit down together for an hour to review one of them. You will probably do a much better job of explaining your comments than you would in writing and, more important, you will show a concern that is likely to improve the writer's attentiveness to her written work.

CHAPTER 10

More Advice for Common Types of Legal Writing

THE ADVICE in previous chapters has been generic: It applies to all types of expository legal writing. This final Chapter discusses some special characteristics of four types of documents: memoranda, briefs, judicial opinions, and letters.

Legal Memoranda

The Basic Structure

While the details of a memorandum's form vary among schools, firms, and legal departments, there is general agreement about its basic structure. In most cases—the exceptions will be examined later—the principles dictate that a memorandum should have the following five elements in the order listed, or bear the burden of justifying its deviation:

Statement of facts. Most memos begin with the facts for two reasons. First, the facts are most likely to be "old" information, knowledge that the reader already has and feels comfortable using as a starting point. In many cases, the facts will have been given to you by your reader (a client or another lawyer), so that by restating them you reassure her that you are starting out in step on common ground, before you lead her into the unfamiliar terrain of your analysis.

Second, the facts provide a necessary context for the analysis that follows: The legal issue must be drawn from the facts and the legal conclusion must demonstrate its relevance to them. The factual context may also help the reader to determine whether cases you cite have been properly relied upon or distinguished, and whether your reasoning by analogy is sound.

To serve these purposes, the statement of facts should be artfully crafted. In most memos, it should be brief. Limit it to the basic factual situation, and bring in more facts later as you need them. In the rarer cases that demand a full description of a complex set of facts to set the context for the issues, impose an order on the facts that helps the reader through them. (See Organizational Technique F on pages 3–22 through 3–25). At times, this order may be simply a clear chronology. At other times, it may derive from some other focal point around which the facts can be organized, such as a series of legal questions, or important gaps or ambiguities in your factual information, or differing standards of judicial review.

Succinct statement of the question or questions. In other words, what do you think this memorandum is about? The statement usually takes one of two forms: a complete sentence ending in a question mark or an incomplete sentence beginning with "whether" that may or may not end in a question mark. We prefer the former. The latter tends to produce sentences that are grammatically convoluted and that diverge unnecessarily from the normal idiom of written English.

Summary conclusion. For each question, supply a summary answer. Of the three introductory sections, this is usually the hardest to write. Watch out for these problems:

❖ The conclusion should address not just the legal questions, but also the practical problem that led the client to consult a lawyer. If you sound as if your horizon is limited to the walls of the library, the result will be extraordinarily frustrating to the reader who has to act on the basis of the answer. This does not mean, of course, that you should usurp the role of the client by offering nonlegal advice, or that you should be too brash in telling a more senior lawyer what advice she should give to the client. But you should almost always push the legal conclusion until it is as practically useful as you can make it.

❖ When you have multiple questions and conclusions, they are often linked by a more general question that may not be stated explicitly:

How should the provisions be drafted? In what forum is the case likely to be tried? What are the tax consequences of the transaction? Be sure to address the general question as well as the specific ones. By doing so, you will usually draw your conclusions toward a practical result, as the preceding paragraph suggested.

If you have more than three questions, incidentally, it is usually clearer to place each answer directly after its question, rather than to set out questions and answers in separate sections. But this detail of form, like many others, may be governed by the conventions of your office or audience.

❖ Summary conclusions tend to be sprinkled with words like "perhaps," "probably," "most likely," and so forth. This caution is often necessary; if the question was difficult enough to require written analysis, the answer is unlikely to be certain. But the qualifications should be as clear and conceptually precise as any other part of the conclusion's content. This means, first, that you should explain why you must hedge. (Is the case law sparse and old? Does the conclusion take a step or two beyond established precedent?) It also means that your reader should know what you think the odds to be. Are you hedging simply to take account of the unpredictability of judges and the complexity of the analysis, or because you are making a close call among competing conclusions? Finally, it means that your hedging should be consistent throughout the memo. In first drafts, especially those written by young lawyers venturing into new areas of the law, it is common to find that the first page's "probably" becomes "perhaps" by the tenth page, or that "the case law suggests" turns out to mean "the case law states firmly, but I couldn't find many cases."

After you have written the facts, question, and summary conclusion, do not assume that you have necessarily provided all the introduction you need. In some memoranda, usually short ones, these sections will be enough. Longer, more complex ones, however, may need a more detailed road map: perhaps a list of the subissues into which your analysis divides, or a description of your analytical "theme" (see page 3–20). This road map can appear at the end of the summary conclusion or at the beginning of the analysis itself. Writing the map requires some tact. It should be clear, of course, but also as brief and as substantive as possible. And it should not belabor the obvious.

Analysis. The discussion of your research and reasoning will now be an explanation—in effect, a defense—of the summary conclusion. Instead of building to a dramatic close that remains hidden until the end, you proceed step by logical step toward a result you have announced in advance. This sequence not only helps the reader grasp the logic of the analysis; it also helps you avoid digressions and non sequiturs.

To make the analysis proceed smoothly from the reader's perspective, make its structure explicit not only at the beginning, but throughout. For example, when you are about to discuss a case or another authority at length, begin by explaining how it will support the analysis.

Conclusion. The initial summary conclusion and the careful analytical defense of it should make any lengthy restatement of your conclusions unnecessary. The only exceptions should be very long memoranda that deserve recapitulation.

Some Exceptions to the Basic Structure

The reasons for using a different structure are usually obvious when they occur, and some have already been noted. If you are writing about a general legal issue, rather than one arising from a set of facts, then, of course, your first section will deal with the issue. At other times, the facts and the question, or the question and the conclusion, may slip so smoothly into each other that it would be clumsy and long-winded to separate them. And, at times, you may dispense with the whole machinery of labeled introductory sections, either because the memo is short or because your client prefers a less formal approach.

Presenting the Analysis: Some Dangers

While we are focusing on memoranda, we will take the opportunity to make some additional points about them that go beyond their organization. These points concern primarily your attitude toward, and thus your presentation of, the analysis section. The first point is the most basic, for it is at the heart of all the others.

Thoroughness. Your reader has the right to rely on your analysis absolutely—to expect that you are willing to stake your professional reputation on it, as she may have to stake hers. This standard has at least three consequences. First, be sure that your research has been exhaustive, a particular concern in these days of Lexis and Westlaw. On these systems, a bad choice of key words or search logic can lead you to miss crucial cases. Second, do an honest job of explaining the weaknesses of your argument and of presenting counterarguments. Third, if you are writing for a more senior attorney, provide enough detail from your sources so that she is able to form her own judgment about the conclusions you have reached. At times, this may require lengthy quotations or the appending of cases and statutory materials.

Objectivity. As we implied in the previous paragraph, a memorandum is not normally advocative or adversarial. It should be evenhanded in its discussion of the strengths and weaknesses of a conclusion or a proposed action. But objectivity is not the same as indifference to a client's interest. It does not necessarily mean that you cease your analysis when you reach the "right answer" from the point of view of the "law" itself. While this would be the proper approach for a detached observer, such as a judge, judicial clerk, or law professor, it is not usually the right one for a practicing lawyer. The practitioner's professional responsibility is to analyze the law objectively, but with the client's goals always in mind. The client expects her lawyer to be an ally, not just a legal technician, and to explore every legal and ethical means of achieving her goal. She deserves the demonstration that all analytical stones have been turned in her behalf, particularly when she does not consider the result to be good news.

Citing case support. Avoid citing cases without some sense of factual context. Your reader will want the most accurate picture of the law possible within the confines of a few pages. She will therefore need to grasp the relationship between the issue at hand and cases you cite but do not discuss in detail. For this reason, "string cites" are rarely helpful. Ordinarily, each citation to a case that is not itself discussed in the text should be followed by at least a short parenthetical to establish its context. Deviate from this pattern only when you are convinced that such information is unnecessary.

Footnotes. Many attorneys consider footnotes to be vile remnants of bad habits introduced by unfortunate experiences on law journals. Others of us feel naked without them. The truth lies, as it usually does, somewhere in between. In most briefs, memoranda, and opinions, footnotes are unnecessary. But there are exceptions:

1. *Citations.* While citations in the text, if not too voluminous, can enhance the effect of a legal argument, they can also weaken it if the reader must struggle with several lines of citation in the midst

of a developing analysis. Put lengthy citations in a footnote instead.

2. *Discussion.* Footnotes should be used to discuss matters not directly to the point of the analysis. Consequently, be wary of using footnotes in documents intended primarily to persuade rather than to demonstrate thoroughness.

By this stage of the book, it should be no surprise that we are offering not a rule about the use of footnotes, but a principle that will lead to different results in different situations. The principle is simple enough: Keep the line of your analysis clear and uncluttered. Given this principle, footnotes are always an inconvenience, because they ask the reader to interrupt her walk down the main path. But sometimes they are the lesser evil.

"Blue-booking" or "Maroon-booking." Attitudes concerning the acceptable form of citation vary widely, from "what the heck, just so they can find the case" to "run this page off again because you put a period after the d in 2d Cir." Many would argue that the best attorneys fall at the latter end of the spectrum, stressing an ethic of professional excellence that includes very high standards for a professional product. In this context, attention to detail—even when the specific detail seems trivial—is likely to be taken as a sign of your acculturation to the profession's standards.

Briefs

A brief transforms the relatively objective analysis of a memorandum into an adversarial argument to a court. The change is important, of course, and it has consequences that are discussed below. But the basic standards of communication remain the same: You must still make your argument clear by the methods described earlier. Advocates win most of their points by clarity and straightforwardness—not, as many novice litigators seem to believe, by demonstrating sincerity or outrage, or by laying down an artillery barrage in the hope that the sheer volume of argument will produce victory.

In what follows, then, we still take our general principles as a foundation. On it, we will erect six more specific principles for writing persuasive briefs.* The first two define how you should approach the court—that is, the attitude you should bring to your argument. The others apply to various parts of a brief.

Candor

We begin where all professional work must: simple honesty. No argument will succeed in the end unless the court is convinced of your credibility. This means that you must demonstrate fidelity to both the facts and the law. Represent the underlying facts or procedural history of the case accurately—you cannot omit relevant facts that are harmful to you, nor can you distort information to your advantage. Acknowledge relevant legal authority even if you will argue against some or all of it. And cite cases both accurately and fairly: Do not refer to cases you know to be irrelevant or unsupportive; and when a case is helpful but not precisely on point, note and deal with the differences. Acknowledge as well the burdens of proof—at the trial level: preponderance of the evidence, clear and convincing, and so on; at the appellate level: clear error, reversible error, abuse of discretion, and so on.

Candor also requires that you understand how much you must concede in an argument. Finally, it requires that you address your arguments to those your opponent raises, not to those that are easier for you to refute.

Comfort

You should ordinarily make the court as comfortable as possible with your argument. In other words, avoid forcing the court to adopt new, difficult, or controversial positions, and instead argue that your result is a natural application or extension of existing law. Conversely, attempt to cast your opponent's arguments as unusual or far-reaching. This means that you usually argue for the narrowest and least adventurous grounds for your result—that is, you should not ask for a result that portends future litigation to clarify the legal situation, nor for one that will affect cases with widely different facts.

---

* The form and most of the content of this section are based on excellent presentations on appellate brief writing by Judge Michael Farrell of the District of Columbia Court of Appeals. We have been fortunate to have shared the podium with him at programs on legal writing, and to have received his permission to use his thoughts here.

In an appellate brief, then, if you are defending the result below, you should assure the judges that the law easily encompasses the trial court's actions (plenty of good evidence; alternative grounds available; no basic unfairness). If you are contesting that result, you want the judges to realize that they need not go out on a legal limb to reverse. In either event, you do not want the court to feel that it must be particularly creative to agree with you. Do not ask the court to announce a new rule, or sharply extend an old one, unless absolutely necessary.

To make the court comfortable, you should also give it reason to believe that your outcome is just. In some cases, of course, judges may feel constrained to reach a result they do not like because statute or case law leaves them no choice. In most cases, though, the law leaves enough room for maneuver so that judges can do justice while still performing a technically correct legal analysis. Without being heavy-handed, show that the result you ask for is equitable as well as correct. While this advice sounds banal, it is often ignored, primarily because a brief-writer is so immersed in research by the time she begins to write that she bogs down in legal technicalities. Step back from the research and look at the case afresh. Many good appellate lawyers go as far as to say that, contrary to the textbook description of appellate argument, facts win the day more often than law—because facts show where justice lies.

Context

In at least one respect, briefs are no different from any other form of effective expository writing: You must map the basics of the situation and your argument before plunging into details. This map has three parts.

State the point. At the outset of your argument, tell the court your contention or "point":

> "The primary issue presented is . . ."

> "The trial court erred in admitting hearsay evidence . . ."

In many jurisdictions, local court rules, particularly at the appellate level, impose a format for phrasing the point, often in an "Issue Presented" section. Consequently, while the point of a memorandum usually appears in a summary conclusion, the point of a brief often has to be packaged first as an issue—though you may have a second chance in a "Summary of Argument" section. If your brief begins with a statement of issues:

❖ You should nevertheless write its final form last. Only after you have developed the full range of your argument can you reduce it to a lucid summary.

❖ Each issue should be stated as an epigram in the form of a rhetorical question. In other words, it should be terse and memorable, and should imply its own answer:

> Can the plaintiff state a *prima facie* case of product defect against an automobile manufacturer when the plaintiff's only evidence at trial was the driver's testimony that prior to the accident the vehicle performed normally?

❖ The issue should embody the appropriate standard of review ("whether the trial court abused its discretion . . .").

❖ It should identify the legal issue ("whether the legislature intended . . .").

❖ It should, if possible, capsulize the key facts that suggest the answer ("whether, in circumstances where plaintiff specifically asked the trial court to do X, plaintiff can fairly complain . . .").

❖ It should state the matter from the litigant's perspective, not from a detached, "judicial" perspective. In other words, tell your client's story ("can the plaintiff reasonably contend . . ."), not the law story ("whether the doctrine of fraudulent conveyance should include . . ."). But do not slant the story so much in your favor that you lose credibility.

Link the point to a road map. If a contention is supported by a sequence of arguments, the context should also include a summary of them. In other words, link the point to a road map. This map can often be drawn—ideally, it should always be drawn—from the way in which you have phrased the issue. As far as possible, it should also have its own internal coherence: Instead of presenting a sequence of loosely related arguments, it should lay out an analysis in which one step leads inexorably to the next. The more complex your analysis, the more important this road map becomes.

For an example of a short but effective road map, look back at the example that begins on page 8–8. This passage is the introduction to a memorandum in support of a motion. Note, first, that it offers a familiar kind of road map, a list of three issues. Then look more closely at the statement of the second issue. It provides a map of the argument that supports the writer's contention—

a map that will guide the writer and reader when the brief returns to this issue. This is the kind of map that brief writers should provide more often than they do.

Present facts with an eye toward the law. Another part of the context for a brief's argument is the statement of facts. To be effective, it must provide the kind of comfort we discussed above: It should prepare the court to appreciate your legal arguments in terms of their results in the real world.

More specifically, bear in mind the following advice:

❖ State only the facts you need, but do not ignore material facts that are harmful to your contentions.

❖ Do not burden the opening statement of facts with details relevant to a specific argument that you will develop in full later. Just state the basics.

❖ Avoid argumentative characterization of the facts. The way you marshal them—their cumulative force—should be sufficient to pave the way for your argument.

❖ Often, the standard of review in the case (reversible error versus sufficiency of the evidence, and so on) will dictate how best to present the facts.

As we stressed in Chapter 2, contexts are necessary at every level within a document, not just in its opening paragraphs or the beginnings of major sections. Context should always precede details of any kind. Thus, you should never discuss a case at length without first explaining its relevance. If the court must wait for the explanation, then you may have already lost the point.

Coherence

Judges often complain that briefs present both facts and legal argument incoherently. Case citations, references to the record, statements of legal doctrine, and so on often have little connection to each other and seem aimless. The problem is usually that the writer has not crystallized in her own mind both the point she wants to make and the interconnections among her subpoints. This clarity can rarely be achieved in a first draft. For a truly coherent argument—one that works cognitively as well as logically—you must step back from the details packed into the draft and integrate all parts of your presentation: The facts lead **toward** the argument, which in turn looks back toward the facts, and each section of the argument leads smoothly to the next.

A well-integrated argument is one you can outline rigorously and summarize succinctly. It is also characterized by patterns or themes that draw your argument together—for example, patterns of unfairness or error whose cumulative impact reinforces each contention. In many instances, then, to make your argument complete and more persuasive, its theme should be based on public policy, justice, or common sense (and, conversely, on the social costs of your opponent's position). To be convincing, of course, your technical legal arguments must be thorough, but that does not mean that you concentrate only on minutiae. Instead, you must also address the broader principles at stake.

For these reasons, the test of an argument's coherence is the writing of the initial paragraphs that set the context for the rest. If you cannot write a clear introduction, then something is wrong with the structure of your argument. But once you do have that statement of context, it will help to steer the reader through the entire argument.

In pursuit of coherence, make the structure of your argument as simple as possible, even if its details are sophisticated and nuanced. It is always impressive to say, for example, "Appellant's contention is refuted by three separate arguments, each of which by itself is sufficient to defeat it." And then use road signs liberally—even such simple ones as "first," "second," and "third"—to keep the court on track.

Two techniques help emphasize the coherence of your argument. The first is the use of headings and subheadings. In a brief, these headings are customarily more than just a few key words, like "I. The Trial Court's Error," or "A. Inappropriate Reliance on *Dees v. Murphy*." Instead, they are summaries of each section's point:

> I. The District Court erred in dismissing Appellant's action for damages on the grounds that a habeas corpus proceeding is an appropriate prerequisite for an action based on *Bivens v. Six Unknown Federal Narcotics Agents.*
>
> . . . .
>
> a. Appellant's *Bivens* action should not be dismissed due to the decision in *Dees v. Murphy* because that case need not, and should not, be followed here.
>
> . . . .
>
> 1. *Dees v. Murphy* is inconsistent with the reasoning in the more recent Eleventh Circuit case of *Gwin v. Snow*, creating a split among panels of the Circuit that allows this Court to consider the matter thoroughly.

These headings should be used rather frequently to avoid forcing the court to wade through lengthy discussions without a break.

A second technique for reinforcing coherence is to remind the court of your themes when you introduce new contentions. Here is an example of a summary recapitulation:

> To this point plaintiff has demonstrated that both the plain language and the purpose of the statute reveal that the legislature did not intend to deny this class of persons the right to vote in these elections. Plaintiff now shows that, were the statute to be read otherwise, it would raise profound constitutional questions.

The goal of a coherent structure is in fact more ambitious than just to show that the writer's thoughts are organized. What you seek is a sense of inevitability—one idea flowing ineluctably into the next, producing a compelling picture of justice. No writer can hope to achieve this impression of irresistibility without paying close attention to coherence.

Compression

Another element of a brief's persuasiveness is its compactness. A well-pruned argument suggests confidence; a long, rambling one suggests desperation, or at least nervousness. A tight, spare presentation is a sign of character.

Each portion of a brief should be squeezed of its excess. Remove unnecessary facts, and do not repeat facts later in the argument section unless they are critical. Discuss cases only when they relate directly to your conclusions. Avoid "string cites" unless you specifically need to impress the court with the weight of authority on a particular point. Most important, do not dilute your argument with weak, thinly supported contentions. More is not necessarily better—stick to your principal points, and keep the court's attention focused.

Your paragraphs and sentences should be equally compact and efficient, of course, but on this point we simply refer you to the earlier chapters of the book.

Collision

Finally, a brief must speak to the issues to be decided by the court. Although this is obvious, there are better and worse ways of doing so.

For example, as a matter of both candor and comfort, it is often useful to announce up front what your argument does *not* involve—to limit and focus your imposition on the court's time. In addition, although you will want to brainstorm the issues before you write so that you consider as many variations as possible, do not burden your argument with every conceivable nuance. Instead, take care in selecting the better points, and arranging them properly, so that you do not squander your credibility.

When you arrange the order of points, ordinarily lead with your best—not in terms of its legal sophistication, but in terms of comfort. That is, give the court the easiest grounds it can use to sustain your position—in an appellate brief, for example, the least difficult or problematic basis for reversal or affirmance. Thus, if you have both a statutory and a constitutional argument, start with the statute. And if you have one argument that relies upon a statute to reach your result and another that invalidates or circumvents the statute, begin with the one that leaves the statute intact.

Special reasons, however, might counsel a different order of argument. For example, the chronology of events may suggest that you raise the issue of suppression of evidence before you focus on other errors at trial. Or you might decide to argue the suppression point first because it has the more fundamental impact, ending the government's case rather than just getting your client a new trial.

A corollary to this principle of priority is that you should ordinarily argue first the strength of your own contentions rather than the weakness of your opponent's. For example, if your case turns on construing a statute that has been interpreted unfavorably to you in other decisions, focus first on the language and purpose of the statute to show that they support your position, and then attack the cases on which your opponent relies. (The well-known, but more extreme, adage here is: "If you don't have the facts, argue the law; if you don't have the law, argue the facts.") All of this advice, however, is subject to the principle of candor, discussed earlier.

Another corollary involves footnotes: Confront the hard issues raised by your opponent in the text of your brief, not in its footnotes. As a general proposition, avoid excessive or lengthy footnotes. In addition to the annoyance they can cause, they can suggest a disingenuous approach to the issues at stake if too much substance is buried in them.

Finally, we think it worthwhile to reiterate some general advice about the tone of your argument. To protect your professional credibility, you should be reasonable and restrained. There is a subtle, but readily noticed, difference between arguing strongly and arguing loudly. You should never disparage the court or your adversary, therefore, nor should you ever overstate your case. And, whenever possible, avoid relying on adjectives and adverbs to emphasize your points (e.g., "clearly," "obviously," "very," etc.). Instead, make substance rule over form: Let the logic and coherence of your presentation create its compelling force without props or fillers.

Judicial Opinions

The principles and techniques discussed earlier apply as much to judicial opinions as to memoranda and briefs, of course. But the opinion serves a different purpose, is addressed to a different audience, and rests upon a different kind of authority. As a result, applying the principles and techniques may lead to different results.

For example, in order to apply the principle of "context before detail" to an opinion, a judge should usually put the issue before the facts, reversing the conventional organization of a memorandum. Unlike the memo writer, the judge is not usually setting out to show that the issue has been properly drawn from the facts because the issue has ordinarily been defined at an earlier stage of the proceeding. Instead, the judge is trying to resolve the issue, by using facts and law which will take on meaning for the reader only because they are relevant to the issue. Thus, the structure of a simple opinion will be:

(1) Introduction, including issue
(2) Facts
(3) Discussion of law
    (a) Proof of right argument
    (b) Rebuttal of mistaken argument
(4) Restatement of conclusions, if necessary, and order, judgment, etc.

While this outline provides an organizational guideline, the principles that created it, being principles, will also require the judge to abandon it occasionally. At times, for example, when the definition of the issue is closely tied to a specific set of facts, the judge may need to describe the facts first to make the issue comprehensible. Occasionally, when the judge will dispose of the case by applying a settled principle or standard of review to the facts, she may want to state that legal background before the facts, because it provides the context in which the facts take on significance. And, frequently, the judge will want to dispose of a wrong argument before stating the right one, either because the right one is controversial, or because its justification rests on the flaws in the wrong one. The principles, not the format, should control the opinion's organization.

In what follows, we concentrate on an opinion's introduction. A good introduction, as we have argued earlier, can do wonders for a reader's—and a writer's—clarity of mind.

Introductions

Although there is no single recipe for an opinion's introduction, there is a universal list of ingredients:

(1) (Trial) Nature of the case and parties involved: who wants what from whom?

(Appellate) Nature of the case, results at trial, and parties involved: who wants what from whom?

(2) Specific issue: What questions must be answered before the judge can decide who gets what?

(3) Decision, and a summary of the reason for it.

(4) Controlling legal principle, statute, standard of review, etc.

The first and second ingredients should be present in most introductions, although in a multi-issue case it often does not make sense to state every issue in the introduction (see page 10–21). The third is usually helpful, as a way of both enlightening and persuading readers. The fourth, on the other hand, is rare, because many cases do not involve a controlling legal standard that can be stated clearly at the opinion's start.

Whatever specific ingredients the introduction contains, it should tell the reader who wants what from whom, and exactly what the fight is about—and the more exactly, the better.

As you decide what the introduction should contain, you face three distinct questions: (1) What should you tell readers to provide a clear overview of the case? (2) What should you tell them to prepare them to understand the significance of the facts (which, presumably, will follow the introduction)? (3) What is most important to the case as it now stands—a novel issue? the background of the dispute? the procedural history?

Some sample introductions appear below. They can serve as models for opinions that deal with one or two issues, or three at most.

> The plaintiff, publisher of a daily newspaper in Smith County, seeks an order requiring Lexington Village, a municipal corporation, and

the chief of its volunteer fire department, Jim R. Jones, to make fire records more readily available.

* * * * *

The City of East Humboldt charged the defendant with violating City Ordinance 305 by failing to obtain a business license for rental property he owns. He was found not guilty by the East Humboldt Municipal Court, which concluded that the ordinance was unconstitutional.

In this appeal by the City, counsel for both parties have stipulated that the matter would be heard on the record without further evidence.

We have two basic questions to consider:

(a) Does Ordinance 305 impose an excise tax, which the City is empowered to collect, or does it impose an income or property tax, which the City may not collect?

(b) Does the ordinance deny the defendant equal protection of the law because it applies only to those who own or operate three or more properties?

* * * * *

Safe Insurance Company sues to recover $78,100 paid under a homeowner's policy after defendant's house was destroyed by fire. We have to decide, first, whether the defendant intentionally set the fire. If we find that he did, we must then decide whether the plaintiff may recover from the defendant money it paid to a mortgagee, or is limited in its redress to foreclosure and suit on the debt afterwards.

* * * * *

Plaintiff, Slick Oil Company, leased a service station to defendant under an agreement that allowed Slick to cancel the lease if defendant owed it over $2,500 for more than 60 days. After canceling the lease because of defendant's debt, plaintiff now sues for possession of the service station and recovery of the debt. We grant judgment upon the debt. We find, however, that plaintiff is prevented by the rules of estoppel and waiver from canceling the lease, because it had been renewed when defendant's debts already exceeded the limit that allowed plaintiff to end the lease.

* * * * *

The Smith County Division of Welfare claims that the plaintiff received welfare payments to which he was not entitled because his mother failed to report a lawsuit in which he has so far been awarded $35,000. The Division asserts a lien against that award to recover the overpayment.

Its claim raises three issues. First, was an over- payment made? If so, does *W.C.S.A.* 44:10-4(a), and the case law interpreting it, authorize a lien to recover the money? If not, can the division rely on an administrative regulation—W.C.A.C. 10:81-3.41(e)(1)—which authorizes a lien despite the lack of statutory authorization?

We find that an overpayment was made, and that the Division is entitled to a lien under the authority of the Administrative Code because the Code is properly designed to enforce the intent of *W.C.S.A.* 44:10-4(a).

* * * * *

Among judges who usually write good introductions, one failing often persists: They describe the issue so broadly that the introduction neither sets up the specific question the opinion must answer, nor shows the reader what to look for in the facts. If the case will be resolved at least partly by the facts, the introduction's statement of the issues should be precise enough to help readers to distinguish crucial facts from background ones and to see how the facts lead toward a conclusion.

In the following three versions of an introduction, for example, only the last states the issues precisely enough:

(1) The City of Cortez appeals from a judgment declaring a special assessment levied against Fast Freight Systems, Inc. null and void. Because it appears from the record that the real controversy in issue has not been fully tried, we reverse and remand the cause to the trial court for a determination of the merits. *See* sec. 752.35, Stats.

* * * * *

(2) The City of Cortez appeals from a judgment declaring a special assessment levied against Fast Freight Systems, Inc. null and void. Because it appears from the record that the real controversy in issue has not been fully tried, we reverse and remand the cause to the trial court for a determination of the merits. *See* sec. 752.35, Stats.

The circuit court granted the judgment because the City's pleadings, filed in response to Fast's appeal of the assessment, did not include material that was a statutorily required part of the assessment process.

* * * * *

(3) The City of Cortez appeals from a judgment declaring a special assessment levied against Fast Freight Systems, Inc. null and void.

> The circuit court granted the judgment because the City's pleadings did not contain a copy of the report on which the assessment was based. While we agree that the report was a statutorily required part of the assessment process, we find that Fast had knowledge of the information it contained, and was therefore not damaged by its omission from the pleadings. Because the real controversy at issue has not been tried, we reverse and remand the case for a determination of the merits. *See* sec. 752.35, Stats.

Now the facts: Judge for yourself which introduction allows you to deal with them most intelligently.

> The undisputed facts reveal the following: On June 17, 1980, Cortez, pursuant to sec. 66.60, Stats., passed a preliminary resolution to install sanitary sewers and declared its intent to exercise its special assessment powers to finance the construction. This action was authorized by its broad police and statutory powers. Fast owns land which has two boundaries that abut the proposed new sewer lines. The common council resolution authorized the director of public works to prepare a report as described in sec. 66.60(2) and (3). That report was to include a schedule of the proposed assessments for each parcel affected. The report was to be filed in the city clerk's office for public inspection.

> A public meeting to consider the assessment was scheduled for August 5, 1980, at 6:30 p.m. in the council chambers. Adequate notice of the meeting was given. The notice itself expressly stated that the report of the director of public works showing the proposed plans and specifications, the estimated costs of the improvements, and the proposed assessments was on file in the director's office and could be inspected during regular business hours. The public meeting was convened at the scheduled time in the municipal building. A representative of Fast was registered as being present. . . .

In a multi-issue opinion, the introduction poses another problem: How many of the issues should it describe? The choice will depend partly, of course, on their number and complexity. An introduction can safely contain four issues if each can be stated in a few words, but it may collapse under the weight of three complex ones. Aside from number and complexity, how the judge handles the issues will depend on the answer to two questions. First, how many of them, if any, are only of secondary importance? Are one or two dispositive? Second, is there a relationship among the issues? Are some of them similar, or does one of them have to be answered before you move on to the others? Depending upon the answers to these questions, the judge can choose one of the following ways of stating the issues in the introduction:

(1) List all the issues.

(2) State the main or dispositive issue; save the rest.

(3) Summarize the kind (or kinds) of issues involved.

(4) List all the issues, but organize the list.

(5) Rather than state or summarize any of the issues, give readers the information they need to grasp what the case is about and to understand the relevance of the facts to be recited. Then state each issue as it is developed.

Examples of choices 2 through 5 appear below.

EXAMPLE FOR (2)

This is an appeal from a conviction in a "battered child" murder case. Husband and wife were tried jointly before a jury, which convicted the wife (appellant) of murder and sentenced her to fifty years. Her husband was found guilty of criminally negligent homicide. Only the wife appeals.

Appellant challenges the sufficiency of the evidence to support the conviction, and raises several other points of error that we will turn to later.

EXAMPLE FOR (3)

Ernest Murphy, the appellant, was indicted for delivering a usable quantity of marijuana of more than one-fourth ounce. The jury convicted him and sentenced him to four years in the West Carolina Department of Corrections. On appeal, he contends the trial court erred in several of its rulings on his objections, motions, and requests. We affirm.

EXAMPLE FOR (4)

Helen Moore filed a motion for an increase in alimony against her ex-husband, James Moore. Moore filed a counterclaim to terminate or substantially reduce alimony. The court increased the alimony and denied Moore's requested relief. Moore appeals. We reverse.

This case presents several interrelated issues. We must first answer three questions about the trial court's right to consider Moore's counterclaim:

(a) May the court disregard a stipulated . . . ?

    (b) Was the provision for alimony . . . ?

    (c) Was a former decision . . . ?

Because we decide these issues in Moore's favor, we must then inquire (d) whether support from a paramour, living with Mrs. Moore as a husband, may be considered on the issue of changed financial circumstances in deciding Moore's right to reduction or termination of alimony. If so, two further questions arise.

    (e) Should alimony have been prospectively reduced . . . ?

    (f) Is Moore entitled . . . ?

EXAMPLE FOR (5)

This appeal is from a judgment sustaining an award of the Workers' Compensation Board, which granted the claimant total disability benefits from an alleged injury. We affirm.

The crucial issues arise from two questions of fact: Did claimant Lewis' injury on the job cause his disability, and is that disability total?

In weighing the evidence bearing on these questions and the more specific issues described later, we abide by the well-settled principle that Workers' Compensation legislation should be liberally construed in favor of the employee [citation]. Given that standard, we find sufficient evidence to support the board's conclusions, despite the presence of conflicting evidence.

Lewis reported to work on March 25, 1977, at 8 a.m. on the job site of Builders, Inc., and began working with a crew employed by John S. Foreman. Two hours later, Lewis developed a kink in his back. At about 2 p.m. he told some employees of Foreman that he was going to a doctor and left the job site. On April 5, 1977, Dr. Smith removed a disc on the right side of claimant's back.

After surgery, he apparently felt well enough to attend the "Firemen's Ball" at the Moose Club on May 14, 1977. On May 22, 1977, after police were called when Lewis became intoxicated at the home of his ex-wife, he hit a deputy sheriff with his motorcycle helmet and proceeded to run his motorcycle into the side of the police car. To restrain Lewis, the deputy sat on him for thirty minutes, during which time Lewis periodically complained about his back. Before these events, Lewis had also been cut with a knife in the stomach in 1968, shot in the chest in 1971, and had his ear cut off in a 1975 automobile wreck.

The Workers' Compensation Board considered the testimony of four medical witnesses and one lay therapist in determining that the claimant was 100% occupationally disabled as a result of an on-the-job injury. On appeal, Builders, Inc. argues:

(1) It was not proven that it employed Lewis at the time of the accident;

(2) Lewis failed to notify his employer of the accident;

(3) Lewis had a preexisting, active, functional disability to which part of the award must be apportioned;

(4) Lewis failed to prove causation.

The Special Fund, to which the Board apportioned 50% of the award, concurs in Builder's fourth argument, and also asserts:

(5) Lewis has not suffered 100% occupational disability.

We will discuss these arguments in turn.

In a multi-issue opinion, a judge often faces a choice about how to handle the facts as well as the statement of issues. The usual method is to describe all the facts after stating the issues. If there are several issues, however, that method often fails because some of the facts are relevant only to individual issues. If all are crammed in near the start of the opinion, the section of facts will not only be unnecessarily long, but many facts will have to be repeated later. In this situation, the facts should be broken up, with only those that set the context for the whole case being described at the beginning.

Organizing Facts and Law

The earlier sections on these topics (see Organizational Techniques D, E, and F on pages 3–18 through 3–25) are particularly relevant to judicial opinions. In particular, when you organize the analysis of an issue, you face three basic choices:

1. Should you state your conclusion at the start?
2. Should you adopt the organization followed by one of the parties, or create a different structure?
3. Should your written organization follow the steps by which you thought through the issue, or take a different approach?

To answer the second and third questions, you should usually break each into two steps. First, did the party's analysis, or your thought process, in fact match the logic of the analysis you finally accepted? If so, you are home free. If not, you face the second step: Should you organize the written discussion so that it matches the structure of the final analysis rather than your thought process? In general, you should. (See pages 3–7 through 3–11.) At times, though, it may be more persuasive to work through the party's mistaken analysis, or your initially misguided approach, so that you can show how you discarded plausible arguments until only the right one remained.

Letters

The category of "letters" includes a range of subcategories. Some letters, such as certain types of opinion letters, are in fact formal legal documents despite carrying a salutation that makes them look like a letter. Other letters are in fact legal memoranda. The line between these "letters" and real letters is fuzzy, but we can try to separate them by means of this distinction: Real letters set out to establish a more direct, personal connection between your mind and the reader's. On the spectrum that runs from a conversation to a statute, a real letter is several steps closer to the conversation than is a brief or memorandum.

As a result, when you write a letter take special care to avoid interfering with that direct link between you and the addressee. Here are the most common obstacles:

(1) Writing in lawyer's jargon or overly formal prose, instead of the common language you share with your audience. This is obviously a mistake when you are writing to a nonlawyer. It is also usually a mistake—or, at least, a lost opportunity—when you are writing to another lawyer because it creates an unnecessarily impersonal, distant tone. Groucho Marx provides this wonderful example:

> Honorable Charles D. Hungerdunger
> c/o Hungerdunger, Hungerdunger & McCormick
>
> Gentlemen?
>
> In re yours of the 5th inst. yours to hand and in reply, I wish to state that the judiciary expenditures of this year, i.e., has not exceeded the fiscal year—brackets—this procedure is problematic and with nullification will give us a subsidiary indictment and priority. Quotes unquotes and quotes. Hoping this finds you, I beg to remain as of June 9th, Cordially, Respectfully, Regards—

Even when you are writing to an adversary, or to the representative of an agency, you can still write directly and simply, as the examples on page 10–25 prove.

The next three obstacles are interrelated.

(2) Failing to make it quickly clear why you are writing and why the recipient should bother to read the letter. In too many letters, especially those

that involve legal analysis, the writer fails to announce how the letter will help the reader or what response the writer wants.

(3) Failing to approach your subject from the reader's perspective, rather than your perspective or the abstract perspective of the law. For example, assume that you are writing about a Supreme Court case that will affect one aspect of a client's business. A lawyer needs no excuse to discuss a major case in detail, and the typical lawyer's letter might begin like this:

> Dear Jane:
>
> Last week, the Supreme Court handed down its decision in *Smith v. Jones* [citation]. This case has several applications to your business, especially to the type of transaction we discussed in June.
>
> In *Smith v. Jones*, the Court overruled . . . .

Here is a better start:

> Dear Jane:
>
> Last June, we discussed your concerns about the regulatory complications that surround transactions in which ABC Inc. . . . . . At that time, the relevant case law provided no help in our attempts to structure the transactions to avoid these complications. Last week, however, the Supreme Court handed down a decision that should be helpful. Specifically, it should allow you to . . . .

(4) Failing to address the reader's implicit concerns as well as the explicit occasion for the letter. If you are writing to explain a settlement or a real estate closing, the recipient probably wants something more than a clear explanation of the technicalities: She wants some sense that you are looking after her interests and that you share her happiness—or frustration—with how matters have gone. In other words, the letter should establish common ground between the two of you.

In addition to the sin of starting off on the wrong foot, two other problems show up frequently in the lawyers' letters we read:

1. Some lawyers have the habit of taking a twenty-page research memorandum, putting it on letterhead, writing "Dear Jane" at the start, and sending it off as a letter. Other lawyers may not wince, but nonlawyers will. If you are sending a client a memorandum, leave it in that format and accompany it with a letter. Ideally, the letter will summarize the memorandum, set it in the larger context

of the client's aims, and, if appropriate, add some kind of personal touch.

2. At the other extreme, many lawyers have the habit of dashing off letters they consider simple and unimportant—for example, transmittal letters that ask the recipient to do something with the documents. The results can approach stream-of-consciousness. If you are sending documents, be sure the recipient understands how they fit into the transaction. If you are asking the recipient to do something, lay out the steps in the order in which they should be taken—not in the order in which you happened to think of them. Here is an example provided in an article on letter-writing by Vee Nelson:

Before:

Dear Jim:

As you requested, we have prepared your deed. It is now ready for signatures. After it is signed, stamped and sealed, it should be returned to our office.

Your signature must be given in the presence of a notary public and a witness. Neither the witness nor the notary can be your kin and both must be over 18 years of age.

Please sign the enclosed deed exactly as your name is printed.

After:

Dear Jim:

As you requested, I have prepared your deed in the form we discussed last month. It is now ready for your signature

Please sign the deed exactly as your name is printed. You must sign it in the presence of a notary public and a witness. Both must be over 18 and unrelated to you.

After the deed is signed and the notary has stamped and sealed it, please return it to our office by hand or by certified mail, return receipt requested.

Below are three more examples of letters that get off to a good start. For a fourth example, see the detailed edit of the "Dear Jane" letter (Example 3) on page 6–10.

EXAMPLE 1

Dear Ms. Jones:

While we were reviewing your interrogatory answers and documents produced pursuant to our document request, we received your motion to withdraw as plaintiff's counsel. Notwithstanding your motion, we thought it preferable to bring to your immediate attention the deficiencies in these responses. If you do not intend to act on them, I suggest that you pass them on to your client.

In discussing your responses to our document request, the numbered paragraphs to this letter will correspond to the numbered paragraphs of our request and your response. . . . .

EXAMPLE 2

Dear Roberta:

Joan Smith and I wish to thank you for providing the opportunity Thursday to discuss ABC's proposed acquisition of XYZ with you and Jane Jones. As we said, both XYZ and ABC are concerned that the issuance of a second request, which would delay the transaction's closing date, would seriously harm the morale of the companies' personnel and could provoke the departure of valuable employees. These consequences would put both companies at a competitive disadvantage.

During our conversation, you indicated that the Justice Department's concerns might be met without a second request if we provided additional information and documentation. We are now providing this material, and we are convinced that it will make clear that the proposed transaction will have no adverse affect on competition or consumer welfare . . . .

EXAMPLE 3

Original:

Dear Ms. Richards:

In reference to your case, please be advised that defendant has agreed to a settlement, the preliminary terms of which are set forth in the document enclosed herein. Prior to the completion of the remaining details of the agreement, this office must be in receipt of the following documentation:

    1. A written estimate from Dr. Jones for the completion of therapy in regard to plaintiff's leg injury.

    2. . . . .

Revision:

Dear Ms. Richards:

As we discussed yesterday, Trust Us Auto Sales has agreed to settle your suit against it. The basic terms are set forth in the enclosed document, which you should review carefully. I believe the terms are favorable, but I urge you to think them through carefully and to phone me if you have any questions.

In order to complete the details of the agreement, I will need the following documents by next Thursday:

1. A written estimate from Dr. Jones for the completion of therapy for your injured leg.
2. . . . .

Coda

WE RETURN TO THE MESSAGE with which the book began. Writing is a craft. Lawyers tend to forget this because, unlike most crafts, this one is learned so early that the process has faded from memory by the end of law school. At some point, most of us stopped thinking about how to write, and simply wrote. Now, however, if you want to improve your professional writing, you must work at it as you would work at improving your ability to ski, play the violin, or cross-examine a witness. Practice the techniques, isolating them and working on them one by one. (But do this when you edit, not when you compose, to avoid blocking the flow of words onto paper.) At first, the effort will feel stiff and awkward, because you will be retraining your mental muscles to break old habits and adopt new ones. Eventually, though, the techniques that are new to your repertoire will come to feel natural. In fact, you will begin to use some of them unconsciously, or half-consciously, when you write first drafts as well as when you edit. In the long run, you will be writing and editing as fluently as you ever did—only better. And, we are convinced, you will be enjoying it more.

APPENDIX A

Justifying Instruction
in Legal Writing

UNFORTUNATELY, WRITING "training" for a lawyer is often nothing more than learning from painful experience that a particular communication has been unsuccessful or poorly received. This should not be characteristic of professional development generally, however, and indeed attitudes have been changing. In recent years, interest in more comprehensive writing training has increased dramatically both in law schools and in the practice, and this text is obviously part of that trend. It is designed to be useful in any context where legal writing is studied, whether by an individual or a group.

Yet the current interest comes saddled with a certain ambivalence. Lawyers, because they are by definition well-educated (or at least much-educated) and often have years of experience producing professional prose, frequently question the usefulness of instruction on a subject as basic as writing. This skepticism cannot be dismissed by simply repeating the popular impression that lawyers write badly and then pointing to a few egregious examples of impenetrable legal prose. Instead, we should take seriously the requirement to justify training in legal writing. By doing so, we might help bring it more into the mainstream of continuing legal education.

Toward those ends, we argue that a good legal writing program is founded on at least the following eight sustaining principles:

1.   The Challenge of Communicating Legal Information

Written communication is precisely that—a form of communication. As we contend in Chapter 1, the goal of professional writing is to transfer information effectively (that is, clearly and persuasively) and efficiently (with the least imposition on the reader). The information with which lawyers are concerned is not, however, a simple laundry list of facts; instead, it is legal analysis, which involves steps in a complex process of reasoning. Good *legal* writing therefore presents that process in a distilled but coherent form. Understood in this way, legal writing is clearly a difficult task that requires more serious study than most lawyers give it.

2.   "Persuasion" as Endemic to Professional Writing

Many lawyers seem to believe that legal writing is produced within separate contexts, each with independent indicia of effectiveness. For example, while briefs are meant to be argumentative and forceful, opinion letters must be cautious and objective. At one level these distinctions are accurate; at another, they are not. At this basic level, all expository legal writing should be "persuasive" in the broad sense of the word. Whatever the context, you will be attempting to persuade the reader of something, even if it is only the completeness of your analysis or the thoughtfulness with which you have approached a client's concern. This is the essence of professionalism: Our responsibility is not just to use our skills and knowledge, but to use them in a way that demonstrates that we are addressing the needs of those for whom we work. This fact reemphasizes the sense of responsibility that all lawyers should bring to the task of communication—and its difficulty.

3.   The Need for a Common Writing Vocabulary in the Editorial Process

The inexperienced lawyer learns the most about the practice of law not from books but from more experienced lawyers. This should be true of legal writing as well. The problem is, however, that lawyers, like the population in general, seem to believe that good writing is more art than science, more a matter of individual "feel" than of principle. Hence, experienced lawyers are often reluctant, or indeed unable, to offer constructive advice to colleagues whose work they must supervise. They will know that a brief or memorandum is not well written, and they will know that their editing has improved it, but they will not be able comfortably and consistently to articulate the reasons. They will struggle with the process of feedback the way the younger colleague struggles with the writing itself. (See the examples of vastly varying editing styles on pages 9–3 through 9–17.)

A good program on legal writing ought to alleviate this problem. It should provide a set of principles and a vocabulary that can serve as the foundation, or at least the starting point, for all conversations about written communication within any organization, whether a law school, a law firm, or a company's in-house legal staff. For newer lawyers in particular, this common vocabulary should enhance, and hasten, at least one aspect of their professional development.

4. Understanding the Relationship Between Style and Substance

One reason for the reluctance to comment on the writing of others is the widely shared belief that differences in writing are more a matter of style than substance. One's writing is held to be as personal and individual as one's taste in clothes.

But this attitude is inconsistent with the degree to which people worry about the opinion others have about their writing. The opposite is closer to the truth: People realize consciously or unconsciously that writing is intimately related to the sophistication of one's intellectual processes. They resent criticism not so much because it seems to be the impertinent substitution of one style for another, but because it feels more like a direct affront to the writer's substantive abilities. A significant edit can be a painful lesson in professional humility or, where the editor is unskilled, an infuriating deterioration of a careful analysis.

A good writing program reduces these tensions by exposing them. Those who believe writing is a matter of style should come to understand the close relationship between style and substance. One's prose can indeed reflect individual characteristics, but what a writer takes to be merely his style can in fact impede communication and therefore become a matter of substance. A good program of legal writing responds to this distinction by giving writers and editors a consistent basis on which to identify it. By anchoring and depersonalizing the process of editorial feedback, the program alleviates much of the discomfort in the discussion.

5. Appreciating the Relationship Between Good Writing and Legal Reasoning

One feature of this book that distinguishes it from others is its explicit attempt to discuss the relationship between writing and legal reasoning. This relationship has several facets. First, as we argue at various points, a lawyer's understanding of the nature and structure of the law will help her understand the similar nature and structure of the principles and rules of effective written communication.

Second, however, this relationship works in the other direction as well. Clear thinking requires clear writing. Language is the vehicle of thought, and no one who writes carelessly can hope to think as well as she otherwise could. As Justice Cardozo emphasized decades ago, in the long run, the quality of our writing affects the quality of our thinking; careful writing clarifies matters for the author as well as the reader. The demands on any lawyer for rigorous thinking are inconsistent with sloppy language.

Third, although the principles of good reasoning and good writing ordinarily yield the same guidance, sometimes they do not. This leads to our next point.

6. Understanding the Nature and Role of Obfuscation

Sad to say, but even murky writing sometimes has its place in legal contexts. Clarity and efficiency are not always the objectives. The best example probably continues to be responses to interrogatories, where passive voice may be preferable for reasons explained earlier in this book. Instruction in writing therefore offers an additional, unexpected dividend. One comes not only to recognize and appreciate the principles of good writing, but also to understand the characteristics of skillful "bad" writing, characteristics that may have more advantages than disadvantages in the proper circumstances. To return to an earlier point, understanding the relationship between writing and reasoning will help one choose the style appropriate to the circumstance.

7. The Need for Efficient Writing Habits

As we suggested in the Introduction, efficient and effective writing should at some point cease being a struggle. However, unless one has more talent than most, good writing can become habitual only if a routine is established based on identifiable, repeatable actions. This demands the kind of principles that writing instruction should provide. And once good writing does become second nature, the principles allow the "natural" writer to explain her talent to those still trying to establish good habits.

8. Recognizing a Public Responsibility

For lawyers whose responsibilities include addressing a public that extends beyond a private client, there is another justification for training in legal writing: The public has a legitimate expectation that it should be able to understand what legal professionals have written. A judge's task, for example, is not simply to decide a case "correctly" according to the law, but to explain that decision clearly and convincingly. Public responsibility and good writing go hand-in-hand.

APPENDIX **B**

A Brief Review of Syntax

MOST OF US WERE TAUGHT grammar so that we could be chastised for our grammatical sins, a process that left us with a hatred of the subject softened only by boredom. But syntax—the part of grammar that has to do with sentence structure—should be more pleasurable to study: Understanding syntax helps us to focus on and control the shapes of our sentences, and it thus leads us towards a more sophisticated, polished style. In this appendix, we provide a naming of the parts of sentences, and of their kinds, so that we can use a common language when we talk about writing good ones.

Parts of a sentence:

A *clause* contains a subject, a verb, and sometimes an object. (In place of the object, you may find what is called a complement: "It is good." or "It is I." Complements appear after "copulative" verbs—that is, verbs that function like an equals sign after the subject.) In other words, a clause has all the parts you need for a grammatically complete sentence. Occasionally, however, one of the parts will be implied rather than present. For example, "Throw the ball" is a complete clause because the subject "You" is there in spirit, although not in body.

An *independent clause* can stand on its own as a sentence. A *dependent clause* cannot, because it begins with a word—such as "because" or "who"—that makes it an appendage of another clause.

A *phrase* is a group of words that forms a unit of meaning but does not amount to a clause. There are many types, some familiar and some rare. For example, we all use prepositional ("in the morning," "to the court") and participial ("running down the street") phrases so often that we do not notice them. Appositives are also common ("the defendant, *a twice-convicted forger*, . . ."). But many writers never use a nominative absolute ("The lawyer, *his argument destroyed by the judge's questions*, . . .").

Types of sentences:

A *simple sentence* contains only one clause (which must, of course, be an independent clause). A *compound sentence* contains two or more independent clauses:

> The winning lawyers smiled for the cameras and the losing lawyer wept.

A *complex sentence* contains one or more dependent clauses (in addition to at least one independent clause):

> After he lost the case, the lawyer shuffled sadly across the street to a bar.

A sentence can be both compound and complex:

> After he lost the case, the lawyer drowned his sorrows at the bar, and then he made the lonely journey back to his empty office.

In a *periodic sentence*, some or all of its basic parts (subject, verb, or object) are withheld until its end, or long after its start, so that no complete thought emerges until you have read all or most of the sentence:

> And all around the sunken sanctuary of the river valley, stretching out in all directions from the benches to become coextensive with the disc of the world, *went uninterrupted prairie.*
>
> Wallace Stegner

There are two kinds of periodic sentences. In the one you have just read, all the basic grammatical parts appear together, once you get to them. In the other kind, they are split up:

> Our *woodpile*, thanks to Henry Allen, who keeps disappearing into the woods mounted on a Cub tractor and towing a small trailer, *has built* to nine cords—mostly birch this year.
>
> E. B. White

In a *loose* (or *cumulative*) *sentence*, all the basic grammatical parts appear first, and then extra phrases or clauses are added. That is, the writer gives you a grammatically complete statement first, before she qualifies or develops it:

> *This was a tiny steel cell*, six feet by six feet, containing two hard, narrow bunks, one above the other—a cute little poky, well off the beaten track.

E. B. White

Clauses within a sentence, as well as the sentence as a whole, can be either periodic or cumulative. Long and fancy sentences will sometimes mix periodic clauses with cumulative ones.

The specific difference between compound and complex sentences is one form of the more general difference between what are sometimes called *paratactic* and *hypotactic sentences*. In a paratactic sentence, phrases and clauses are joined mostly in a coordinate structure—that is, as clauses in a compound sentence are joined, with each getting equal billing. In a hypotactic sentence, phrases and clauses are subordinated to other phrases or clauses—as other clauses are subordinated to the main clause in a complex sentence.

Hypotactic sentences are harder to write (and read) than paratactic ones, because they ask us to sort out the relations among pieces of information that have different degrees of grammatical importance. (Similarly, periodic ones are harder than loose ones, because the former ask us to hold information in suspense until a complete thought finally emerges.) Over the past century, as our tastes have moved toward a simpler, more conversational style, "difficult" sentences have become less frequent even among sophisticated stylists than they were in the nineteenth century and before. (And, of course, sentences have become shorter.) Here is Oliver Goldsmith in the eighteenth century:

> While his youth countenances the levity of his conduct, he may thus earn a precarious subsistence; but when age comes on, the gravity of which is incompatible with buffoonery, then will he find himself forsaken by all; condemned, in the decline of life, to hang upon some rich family whom he once despised, there to undergo all the ingenuity of studied contempt, to be employed only as a spy upon the servants, or a bugbear to frighten children into duty.

And here, in the nineteenth century, is Charles Lamb manipulating an even more complex style, but now with a self-conscious air:

> When my friend commences upon one of those solemn anthems, which peradventure struck upon my heedless ear, rambling in the side aisles of the dim Abbey, some five-and-thirty years since, waking

a new sense, and putting a soul of old religion into my young apprehension—(whether to be *that*, in which the Psalmist, wary of the persecutions of bad men, wisheth to himself dove's wings—or that other which, with a like measure of sobriety and pathos, inquireth by what means the young man shall best cleanse his mind)—a holy calm pervadeth me.

Not all writing in English before our time is this elaborate, of course. In the history of English prose there has usually been a contrast between simple and complex styles. In recent decades, the change has been that a writer who likes to pack a lot of information into his sentences will write loose, paratactic ones to an extent that an earlier age would have considered degenerate. Here, for example, is E. B. White, one of the best modern writers of the personal, informal essay:

> There was a lead editorial in the paper complaining that there had been a drop in out-of-state hunting licenses and urging that Maine get busy and appropriate more money for development, to attract hunters to the state. The theory is that if you shoot forty thousand deer one year you aren't getting ahead unless you shoot fifty thousand the next, but I suspect there comes a point where you have shot exactly the right number of deer. Our whole economy hangs precariously on the assumption that unless more stuff is produced in 1958 than was produced in 1957, more deer killed, more automatic dishwashers installed, more out-of-staters coming into the state, more heads aching so they can get the fast, fast relief from a pill, more automobiles sold, you are headed for trouble, living in danger and maybe in squalor. If that theory is sound, Maine won't be in a solid position until we kill at least forty million deer and with a good prospect of making it fifty million the following year. But that would be the end of the wilderness, and without its wilderness Maine would feel awfully naked.

Notice how much use White makes of "and" and "but," the simplest and most common conjunctions, the most primitive ways of joining two independent clauses into a sentence. Notice also, however, that among all these rambling conversational sentences, just as the style might start to bore us, in the third sentence ("Our whole economy . . .") he offers a piece of stylistic pyrotechnics.

Index

References are to pages and Appendixes

B

C

D